T0305675

Machine Learning for Managers

Machine learning can help managers make better predictions, automate complex tasks and improve business operations. Managers who are familiar with machine learning are better placed to navigate the increasingly digital world we live in. There is a view that machine learning is a highly technical subject that can only be understood by specialists. However, many of the ideas that underpin machine learning are straightforward and accessible to anyone with a bit of curiosity. This book is for managers who want to understand what machine learning is about, but who lack a technical background in computer science, statistics or math.

The book describes in plain language what machine learning is and how it works. In addition, it explains how to manage machine learning projects within an organization.

This book should appeal to anyone that wants to learn more about using machine learning to drive value in real-world organizations.

Paul Geertsema is an academic and consultant in the areas of finance, data science and machine learning. His research involves the application of contemporary machine learning methods to solving problems in finance and business. He teaches Modern Investment Theory and Management (final-year undergraduate) and Financial Machine Learning (postgraduate) at the University of Auckland. Dr Geertsema has published in numerous international peer-reviewed journals, including the *Journal of Accounting Research* and the *Journal of Banking and Finance*, and serves on the board of the AI Researchers Association. Prior to his return to academia, Dr Geertsema worked at Barclays Capital as a derivatives trader in Hong Kong and as a sell-side research analyst in London.

"If you are considering implementing machine learning in your business but don't know where to start, this is the right book for you. *Machine Learning for Managers* is a comprehensive but non-technical introduction to the topic with many relevant examples and implementation guidelines. The split into a detailed overview and project management instructions is ideal for readers who don't have the time to acquire programming skills but are passionate about leveraging AI to enhance business performance. The author's very engaging writing style makes reading a book about a potentially very dry topic enjoyable."

Christoph Schumacher, *Professor of Innovation and Economics; Director Knowledge Exchange Hub, Massey University, New Zealand*

"This book fills an important gap between pure-technical and pure-managerial descriptions of machine learning (ML). Written in a no-nonsense light-hearted style, it is easy to follow, yet doesn't shy away from using technical terms that are important for managers to be able to speak to their ML engineers. Highly recommended for managers looking to understand more about what is under the hood of ML."

Tava Olsen, *Professor, Deputy Dean, Melbourne Business School*

"*Machine Learning for Managers* is a safe haven for non-technical readers interested in understanding what AI and specifically ML is about. With clear, direct and witty language, Geertsema ensures that our journey into AI is like a walk in the park. It is easy, pleasurable and refreshing in its approach and powerful in its choice of illustrations. It brings to the forefront key concepts such as explainability, governance and business case making the message lucent and highly applicable to managers interested in incorporating ML into their business. As a practitioner focussed on human centric AI, I am particularly keen in bringing down AI/ML from its ivory tower status. This book is exactly a tool for this as it provides transparency, deciphers otherwise perceived complex language and is the basis for what ML should do best: to serve you. By far the best introductory ML roadmap I have come across. A must read."

Jose Romano, *Senior Manager at the European Investment Fund and former Entrepreneur in Residence at TAZI.AI*

"The two complementary parts of the book form a comprehensive and practical guide to machine learning. The first part provides a nontechnical overview of machine learning algorithms, demystifying the jargon in the field, which is crucial for students, lecturers and practitioners aiming to apply machine learning to resolve real-life business problems. The second part insightfully examines how machine learning outcomes can be developed and deployed in the organisation's processes. A recommended work for anyone looking to successfully manage the tsunami of big data!"

Leo Paas, *Professor, The University of Auckland Business School;*
Program Director, Master of Business Analytics

"This book provides an outstanding introduction to machine learning from a management perspective. It gives a very clear presentation of the state-of-the-art machine learning methods and how to manage machine learning projects efficiently. It brings a fresh, unique focus on how to learn machine learning from a business perspective. It is highly practical and discusses in detail how a machine learning project should be deployed in real business applications. Not to be missed by any manager with a serious interest in AI and Machine Learning."

Albert Bifet, *Professor, Director of the AI Institute,*
The University of Waikato, New Zealand

Machine Learning for Managers

Paul Geertsema

Routledge
Taylor & Francis Group

LONDON AND NEW YORK

Designed cover image: © Getty Images

First published 2023
by Routledge
4 Park Square, Milton Park, Abingdon, Oxon OX14 4RN

and by Routledge
605 Third Avenue, New York, NY 10158

Routledge is an imprint of the Taylor & Francis Group, an informa business

© 2023 Paul Geertsema

The right of Paul Geertsema to be identified as author of this work has been asserted in accordance with sections 77 and 78 of the Copyright, Designs and Patents Act 1988.

British Library Cataloguing-in-Publication Data
A catalogue record for this book is available from the British Library

Library of Congress Cataloging-in-Publication Data
Names: Geertsema, Paul, author.
Title: Machine learning for managers / Paul Geertsema.
Description: First Edition. | New York: Routledge, 2023. |
Includes bibliographical references and index. |
Identifiers: LCCN 2022057724 | ISBN 9781032362434 (hardback) |
ISBN 9781032362427 (paperback) | ISBN 9781003330929 (ebook)
Subjects: LCSH: Industrial management—Technological innovations. |
Machine learning. | Organizational effectiveness.
Classification: LCC HD45 .G384 2023 | DDC 658—dc23/eng/20230213
LC record available at https://lccn.loc.gov/2022057724

ISBN: 9781032362434 (hbk)
ISBN: 9781032362427 (pbk)
ISBN: 9781003330929 (ebk)

DOI: 10.4324/9781003330929

Typeset in Optima
by codeMantra

Access the Support Material: www.routledge.com/ 9781032362427

Dedication

This book is dedicated to Helen, Simon, David and Heidi. Thanks for your support and understanding!

Dedication

Contents

Contents

Overview

Machine learning is a transformational technology, comparable in impact to electricity, computers or the internet. To benefit from machine learning, you must be able to identify opportunities where it can be applied profitably. This requires an understanding of how machine learning works, what it can and cannot do, and how it can be used to create value in the context of a wider organization. That is what this book delivers. No prior knowledge of higher mathematics, statistics or computer science is assumed.

The core ideas and insights that underpin machine learning are accessible to anyone with a bit of curiosity and motivation. Let me show you how the magic works!

Preface

Most books on machine learning (ML) and artificial intelligence (AI) fall into one of the two categories. Books in the first category are aimed at explaining the importance of AI to a general audience, including senior decision makers such as CEOs. There are many excellent books that explain how AI relates to corporate strategy, innovation and ethics, to name but a few.[1] But after reading these books you still won't know how ML actually works, or how to manage the implementation of an ML system.

Books in the second category are directed at academics or software engineers with specific technical backgrounds. The main thing you learn from reading these books is that you lack the required technical background. Again, many of these books are excellent – provided you have the right technical background.[2]

Machine Learning for Managers covers the middle ground. It is complementary to the general interest and technical books, rather than a replacement for them. *Machine Learning for Managers* explains what ML is, how it works, how to get value from it and how to manage its implementation – in the real world.

There are some things that this book is *not*. It is not a treatise on the theoretical foundations of ML. It is not a guide to coding state-of-the-art, industrial strength enterprise AI systems from the ground up. It is not a finely argued philosophical tract on the relationship between consciousness, intelligence and agency. Above all, this book is not breathless hype. If you have read this far, you already know that ML is important. So we can skip straight to explaining how machine learning works, and how to make it work for *you*.

Writers are often advised to avoid jargon – technical terms – whenever possible. I do not follow this advice. I use established ML terminology copiously, always being careful to explain terms when they are first used. Familiarity with terminology allows you to communicate with experts in their native language. ML engineers talk about *feature engineering*, *hyper-parameter tuning* and *loss functions* all the time – it is as central to what they do as spark plugs and oil filters are to a mechanic.

I had to resist the temptation to write in an academic style. As a result, I do not attribute inventions, innovations and interpretations. Nor do I cite the relevant literature. (A couple of minutes with a search engine is all you need if you really want to know who to credit for a particular algorithm, approach or advance.) Overly technical or mathematical details are tucked away in the notes. It goes without saying that I did not invent the material I explain in this book. My only contribution is to explain ML in a way that is helpful to people who need to get things done, not just talk about it. Enjoy the ride!

Paul Geertsema
Auckland, October 2022

Notes

1   *"Competing in the Age of AI: Strategy and Leadership When Algorithms and Networks Run the World"*, by Marco Iansiti and Karim Lakhani is an excellent introduction to the strategic implications of AI.

2   *"Hands-On Machine Learning with Scikit-Learn, Keras, and TensorFlow: Concepts, Tools, and Techniques to Build Intelligent Systems"*, by Aurélien Géron is a best seller for a reason. This is an excellent starting point if you are already proficient at software development, and now want to start building machine learning systems yourself.

List of figures

List of tables

Author

Dr Paul Geertsema is an academic and consultant in the areas of finance, data science and machine learning. His research involves the application of contemporary machine learning methods to solving problems in finance and business. He teaches Modern Investment Theory and Management (final-year undergraduate) and Financial Machine Learning (postgraduate) at the University of Auckland Business School. Prior to his return to academia, Dr Geertsema worked at Barclays Capital as a derivatives trader in Hong Kong and as a sell-side research analyst in London. Previously he held positions at Credit Suisse as a risk analyst and at Citibank as an IT project lead. His academic background includes a B. Accounting degree, certification as a Chartered Accountant, a B.Sc. in Computer Science, an MBA from London Business School, a Master of Management (Economics) and a PhD in Finance. Dr Geertsema is a founding member of the Artificial Intelligence Researchers Association, where he serves on the board, and a professional member of the Association for Computing Machinery.

Part I

Understanding machine learning

Let's jump right in

It is easy to become lost in a maze of abstractions when we talk about machine learning. For that reason it is a good idea to ground our initial discussion in something concrete. Figure 1.1 provides an example of machine learning in action. It consists of 34 lines of *Python code*. Before you panic, you don't need a background in programming to follow this discussion! Instead I will use the code to make a few important points about machine learning (ML). To provide context, the code in Figure 1.1 uses ML to predict the status of loans (performant or delinquent) by training a model on a data set of historical loans.

1.1 What can we learn from 34 lines of code?

So, what can we learn from the code in Figure 1.1?

ML *is* code. When you dive right through all the abstractions, what you find at the bottom of it all is computer code. Whenever ML is used, it means code is executing on hardware, somewhere. The code may be complex, but there is nothing mysterious about it.

ML tools exist (lines 3–7). Use them. The code imports a selection of Python *packages*. These packages do all the heavy lifting. That is why we can do real ML in 34 lines of code. The moral is simple – do not reinvent the wheel. Before you build something *always* check whether someone has done it already. Most of the best ML tools are open source, and therefore available for use at no cost to you or your organization.[1]

ML requires data (lines 10–11). Without data there is nothing to learn from. More to the point, the quantity and quality of data that you have (or can get) will largely determine the limits of what you can achieve with ML.

DOI: 10.4324/9781003330929-2

```python
 1  # Python code
 2  # import packages
 3  import pandas as pd
 4  import statsmodels . api as sm
 5  from sklearn . tree import DecisionTreeClassifier
 6  from sklearn . model_selection import train_test_split
 7  from sklearn . metrics import accuracy_score
 8
 9  # get data
10  df = sm . datasets . get_rdataset ("loans_full_schema",
11      "openintro"). data
12  df ["performant ] = df [ loan_status"]. apply (lambda x:
13      1 if x in [" Current ", " Fully Paid "] else 0)
14  df = df [["performant ", "emp_length ", "annual_income",
15      "debt_to_income" , "loan_amount"]]. dropna ()
16  y = df [" performant "]
17  X = df [[ "emp_length" , " annual_income " ,
18      " debt_to_income" , " loan_amount" ]]
19
20  # split data into training and test data
21  X_train , X_test , y_train , y_test = train_test_split(X , y,
22      random_state=42)
23
24  # specify and fit model
25  model = DecisionTreeClassifier ( max_depth =3)
26  model . fit (X_train , y_train)
27
28  # predict with model
29  y_test_predicted = model . predict ( X_test )
30
31  # evaluate model
32  accuracy = accuracy_score ( y_test , y_test_predicted )
33  print ( accuracy ) # prints 0.985191637630662
34  print ( y_test .mean ()) # prints 0.985191637630662
```

Figure 1.1 An example of machine learning code

Clever algorithms and powerful computers will also help, but cannot really compensate for a lack of good data.

Most of the effort in ML involves data (lines 12–18). Most ML tools are generic (and readily available for use), but data is usually specific to the application. Because of that, most of the effort and cost of an ML project is driven by the sourcing, cleaning, validating and structuring of data.

In ML we split data (lines 21–22). We train ML algorithms on one set of data (the *training data*) but then test it on another set of data (the *test data*).

The reason is that ML algorithms are powerful enough to model both the patterns *and* the randomness in the training data. The first is desirable, but the second is not. By testing the trained model on test data that the ML has never seen before, we get a better idea of the true performance of the model. (It is for the same reason that students are usually tested on exams that they have not seen in advance.)

What is your problem? (lines 16–17). It is essential to be clear about the problem you are trying to solve. In this case we want to predict loan status, which can be either performant (1) or delinquent (0). By convention the quantity or outcome we are trying to predict – called the *target* – is denoted by *y*. The data we use to make the prediction – called the *features* – are collected in *X*.

Models must be *specified* (line 25). We use a "DecisionTreeClassifier" – just one of a dozen or so ML approaches one could use for this problem. Each approach typically allows one to change various settings (also known as *hyper-parameters*). In line 25 we specify a maximum tree depth of 3 (`max_depth=3`). Both the ML approach and its settings must be specified *before* a model can be trained.

Models must be *trained* (line 26). It is the training process that puts the *learning* in ML. In a nod to the statisticians, it is also referred to as *fitting* a model. In a nutshell, the ML algorithm keeps adjusting its own internal parameters in such a way that performance keeps improving on the training data. We will explain how different ML approaches accomplish this later in the book.

Models must be *evaluated* (lines 34–33). In this case we are calculating the accuracy of the model. Accuracy is simply the percentage of correct predictions. The accuracy of the trained model is around 98.5%, which seems impressive.

Models must be *compared* (line 34). If we simply predict that *every* loan will be performant, then we also obtain an accuracy of 98.5%! This is because 98.5% of loans in the test data set are in fact performant. Line 34 performs this calculation – since performant loans are set equal to one and non-performing loans are set equal to zero, the average value of *y* in test data is also the fraction of loans that are performant. Our model has simply "learned" to predict that a loan will always be performant. (It is a bit like predicting that there will never be an earthquake. Earthquakes are rare. You are bound to be right almost all the time.) The lesson is simple – performance is relative, not absolute. In addition, there are many potential pitfalls when doing machine learning. This illustrates one of them.

1.2 Fitting ML into the big picture

Now that you have seen a concrete example of ML, it is a good time to step back and look at the bigger picture. What is ML and AI – and how does it relate to deep learning, big data, data science, blockchain, fintech and decentralized finance? These terms are often lumped together, but there are important distinctions to be made. Figure 1.2 shows how it all fits together.

Artificial Intelligence is a branch of *Computer Science*. Broadly speaking AI means any artificial system that can accomplish tasks that are thought to require intelligence if performed by a human.[2] Those tasks might be quite narrow, like playing a video game or predicting the sales of different products over the next month. This kind of AI is a reality today.

Machine Learning is a specific AI approach, standing alongside other approaches such as first-order logic, hierarchical planning and so on. Machine learning has become prominent due to its success at a range of problems that were previously considered difficult to solve, such as automatic translation and image recognition. The basic insight that underpins machine learning is that code need not be fixed and static, but can contain internal bits and pieces – *parameters* – that can be changed by the code itself in order to improve its performance. ML algorithms operate by searching for parameters that yield good performance at a particular task. This is the training or learning part of machine learning.

Deep Learning is a specific ML approach that uses neural networks with multiple layers. (The "deep" in deep learning refers to the depth of the layers in the neural network.) While the original work on neural networks were inspired by the neural architecture of the human brain, modern neural networks are best thought of as general-purpose statistical approximation machines. Deep learning is behind most of the high-profile success stories in machine learning, in particular those dealing with unstructured data such as sound, natural language, images or video.

Data Science is a new term that refers to the old practice of empirical science, that is, extracting insights from data. The astronomer Johannes Kepler was acting as a data scientist when he used astronomical observations made by Tycho Brahe to discover that planetary orbits are elliptical back in 1609. There is an inside joke that data science is applied statistics, except that you do it in San Francisco. While there is more than a little truth to the joke, data science also claims ML as a sub-discipline, and so casts a wider net than classical statistics.

Big Data refers to a set of techniques for dealing with large data sets. Both data science and computer science claim big data as a sub-area. There is no real consensus on how big a data set needs to be before it qualifies as "big data". For some, big data is any data set that won't fit in a spreadsheet. For others it is only big data if it won't fit on a single computer. By the latter definition a terabyte of data (roughly a trillion bytes) is not big data, but a petabyte (roughly a thousand trillion bytes) might be. Perhaps the best approach is to call it big data if you actually need to use big data techniques to manage data across many connected computers. Big data and machine learning are different techniques that might from time to time be combined to solve particular problems. One can apply ML to big data, but one can also apply ML to smaller data sets. Similarly, one can use big data techniques to solve problems without making use of ML.

Blockchain refers to a technology that allows for the immutable storage of information without the need for a single source of authority. Blockchain technology underpins both crypto assets such as Bitcoin and Ethereum as well as various decentralized autonomous organizations (DAO's) which in turn underpins Decentralized Finance (or DeFi) initiatives. The main thing that blockchain and machine learning have in common is that they are both newly promising computer-based technologies subject to a certain degree of hype and publicity.

1.3   A layered perspective of machine learning

Figure 1.2 explains how various technologies and approaches relate to each other. But there is another perspective that is perhaps even more important. That perspective relates ML to society as a whole, as set out in Figure 1.3. A vastly simplified, but still useful, approach is to relate the ML code to society via a nested hierarchy of intermediate levels. Implementing machine learning solutions require an awareness of each of the levels. It is particularly at the higher levels – beyond the technical layer of data, code and algorithms – that managers can add value to organizations.

As we have seen, at the very lowest level ML is code applied to data. The code, in turn, embodies various algorithms while the data is generated by

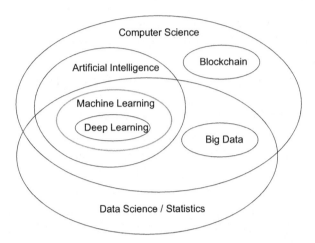

Figure 1.2 How it all fits together – Machine Learning and AI in the wider context

real-world processes. This is the *technical layer*. Part I of the book deals with understanding ML systems at the technical layer.

The code is written by people (sometimes called programmers, coders or developers) while the processes that capture data might also involve people. These people collaborate to solve a particular problem. This is the *project layer*.

A project is normally embedded within a larger organization. Usually it is the organization that provides the resources required by the project. In turn, the organization expects to benefit from the project. This benefit does not have to be monetary (although it often is for commercially oriented organizations). A charitable organization may invest in an ML project if it helps to advance its aims. Publicly funded medical research is one example. The project will need to navigate the internal policies, economic constraints and political tensions within the organization. This is the *organizational layer*.

Organizations themselves function within the context of industries, markets, legal jurisdictions and societies. Some organizations compete while others collaborate; some manage to do both at the same time. It is important to emphasize that society provides organizations with a *license to operate* only insofar it comply with the laws and rules of society. That is to say, society allows organizations a certain degree of autonomy because society expects to benefit from this arrangement (at least on average, if not in every particular case). This is the *societal layer*. Part II of the book explains how ML systems interact with the project, organizational and societal layers.

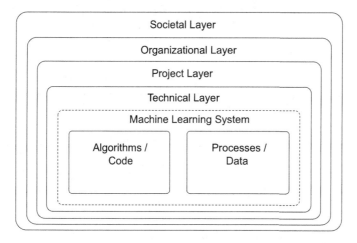

Figure 1.3 A layered perspective of machine learning

1.4 Data, compute and methods

The discussion above placed ML in its wider technological and societal perspective. We now turn to a different question: why is it that ML has suddenly become such a prominent technology?

The short answer is that ML now works; not just in the classroom or the lab, but in the real world. The reason for this can be summarized as better *data*, better *processing power* and better *methods*. Let's consider each in turn.

ML needs data, and we generate more data today that at any other point in our history. The adoption of computers, the internet, mobile phones, social media, cheap sensors and internet-of-things has created a deluge of data. This data is the raw material from which ML systems are fashioned.

Vast amounts of data are not that useful if it cannot be processed. Fortunately a steady increase in computer power has kept pace with the growth in data. Moore's Law states that the number of transistors on a computer chip doubles every year. In practical terms it means the world had benefited from a steady exponential growth rate in processing power since the mid-1960s. Around the mid-2000s researchers started to re-purpose the graphics processing units (GPUs) used by PC gamers to train neural networks. The processing cores in GPUs are slow compared to those found in the central processing units (CPUs) which powers laptops and desktops – but a GPU contains thousands of these processing cores.[3] This steady increase in computing power has enabled ever more powerful ML models.

Figure 1.4 plots the largest ML models for each year over the past four decades, reporting for each year the number of data points on which the model was trained (Graph A), the number of model parameters (Graph B) and the total computing resources required to train the model (Graph C).[4] Each of the graphs are plotted on a logarithmic scale. The number of data points (a proxy for data availability) and the number of parameters (a proxy for model complexity) grew at an annual compound rate of around 65% per year. By contrast, the required computations grew much faster, at an annualized rate of 175%.

In addition to more data and more powerful computers, there has also been a series of innovations and breakthroughs in ML algorithms over the last two decades. A description of these algorithmic improvements would by necessity be fairly technical. Instead I will simply list a few of the more prominent innovations and leave it to the reader to investigate further or skip according to their interests and time constraints. Some of the more important innovations are: (1) in the context of neural networks – rectified linear units (ReLu), dropout, batch normalization, max pooling, new initialization schemes, sparse representations, convolutional neural networks (CNN's), recurrent neural networks (RNN's), generative adversarial networks (GAN's) and attention-based transformer architectures; (2) in the context of tree-based methods – gradient boosting, extreme gradient boosting, histogram methods, gradient-based one side sampling (GOSS) and exclusive feature bundling (EFB). It is absolutely fine if you don't know what any of this means. The main point is simply that many ML algorithms today are far more capable than they were even a few years ago.

Something else has changed over the past two decades. ML is now a mission-critical part of several large and very profitable companies. Table 1.1 lists the 15 most valuable firms globally (as of 22 June 2022). In addition to their market capitalization I also indicate how central AI/ML is to their core operations; either core, supporting or occasional. For firms like Apple, Microsoft, Alphabet (Google), Amazon and Meta (Facebook) the centrality of ML is obvious. Tesla depends on AI for the self-driving features of its cars. Tencent is a Chinese technology and entertainment conglomerate that use AI in its social networks, e-commerce offerings and payment

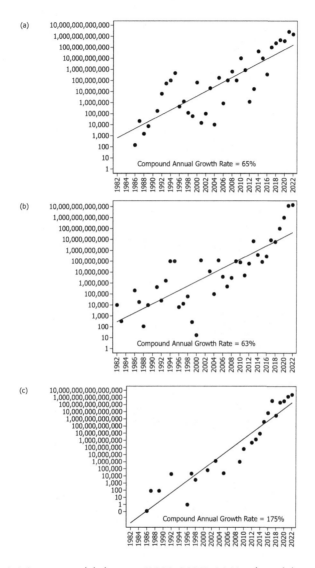

Figure 1.4 Largest models by year (1981–2022). (a) Number of data points, (b) model parameters, and (c) compute (billions of operations)

systems. TSMC is a leading semiconductor company that manufactures AI-specific hardware alongside the more general-purpose processors used in computers and mobile phones. NVIDIA is another semiconductor company whose primary product are the GPU's used in ML, crypto-currency mining and, of course, gaming.

Table 1.1 Drivers of wealth creation – top-15 companies by market capitalization

Company	Size ($ bn)	Centrality of AI/ML		
		Core	Supporting	Occasional
Apple	2,199	✓		
Saudi Aramco	2,198			✓
Microsoft	1,898	✓		
Alphabet (Google)	1,470	✓		
Amazon	1,106	✓		
Tesla	737	✓		
Berkshire Hathaway	600		✓	
Tencent	469	✓		
Johnson & Johnson	455			✓
TSMC	451		✓	
UnitedHealth	451		✓	
Meta (Facebook)	425	✓		
NVIDIA	413	✓		
Visa	411		✓	
Exxon Mobil	385			✓

Note: Valuations are as of June 2022.

1.5 ML drives wealth creation

This means there are now billions of dollars being directed at generating more and better data, creating more powerful compute platforms and improving algorithms and frameworks. A few million dollars a year will keep a field of research alive, but hundreds of billions of dollars a year will drive it forward at speed. That is the current reality for AI research generally and ML specifically. The implication is that this growth in data, compute and algorithms is likely to persist for the foreseeable future.

There is one final point to make before we head to the next chapter. Much emphasis is placed on ML systems that achieve high performance in terms of accuracy or other model-specific measures. It needs to be stressed, however, that an accurate ML system won't necessarily be a valuable ML system. Conversely, an ML system with run-of-the-mill performance could nonetheless generate vast value if it solved the right problem for the right organization. Thus the emphasis should be on identifying those areas where there is value to be added in the first instance, rather than squeezing another fraction of a decimal point out of a performance metric.

Notes

1   Some of the better-known machine learning frameworks are Scikit-Learn, Tensorflow, Keras and Pytorch. These frameworks are usually accessed through the Python programming language.

2   To get a sense of what AI covers you can refer to the outline of *"Artificial Intelligence: A Modern Approach"* by Russell and Norvig. See http://aima.cs.berkeley.edu/contents.html

3   The NVIDIA RTX-3090 contains 10,494 CUDA cores, each capable of executing a simple set of instructions in parallel.

4   Source: https://towardsdatascience.com/parameter-counts-in-machine-learning-a312dc4753d0.

2 | Different kinds of ML

2.1 An introduction to the ML zoo

There exists a vast array of different ML algorithms, much like the animal kingdom. When it comes to animals, we make various distinctions. We could class animals as terrestrial or aquatic. Or to make a more practical distinction, dangerous animals vs non-threatening animals. In each case we are lumping together different animals based on some characteristic. We will now proceed to do the same for ML algorithms. Just as there are tricky cases in the animal kingdom (is a penguin terrestrial or aquatic? is a domestic dog dangerous or non-threatening?), ML algorithms won't always fit neatly into the categories we outline.

In the discussion that follows it might be helpful to refer to Table 2.1 to keep track of the different ways in which we "cut and dice" ML algorithms. Table 2.1 sets out a simple hierarchy of a few common ML approaches. This is not an exhaustive list; there are dozens of ML approaches and thousands of implementations.

2.2 Supervised vs unsupervised ML

The first distinction is between algorithms that predict something (*supervised learning*) and those that do not (*unsupervised learning*).

In supervised learning we are trying to predict a target variable y using a set of features X. The data is a combination of y and X – the objective is to learn some way to predict the target y using only the features X. It is called supervised learning because the algorithm expects to be provided

DOI: 10.4324/9781003330929-3

with examples of the "right answer", in the form of training data that contains the target to be predicted.

Within supervised learning we make a distinction between predicting the type or class of something (called a *classification task*) or predicting a number (called a *regression task*).[1] An example of a regression task would be predicting next quarter customer demand (a number) using historical data. Classifying loans as high risk or low risk (a class) based on accumulated experience is an example of a classification task. In both classification and regression tasks, we expect the supervised learning algorithm to learn how to predict the right answer using training data *where the right answer is provided*.

Table 2.1 A simple hierarchy of machine learning approaches

SUPERVISED LEARNING (prediction)
- **Regression (predict a number)**
  - *Linear models*
    * Linear Regression
    * Ridge
    * Lasso
    * ElasticNet
    * PLS Regression
  - *Tree-based models*
    * Decision Tree Regressor
    * Random Forrest Regressor
    * Gradient Boosting Regressor
  - *Neural networks*
    * MLP Regressor
- **Classification (predict a class)**
  - *Linear models*
    * Logistic Regression
  - *Tree-based models*
    * Decision Tree Classifier
    * Random Forrest Classifier
    * Gradient Boosting Classifier
  - *Neural networks*
    * MLP Classifier

UNSUPERVISED LEARNING (no prediction)
- **Clustering (group things together)**
  - K-Means Clustering
  - Hierarchical Agglomerative Clustering
- **Dimension reduction (compress features)**
  - Principal Component Analysis

In unsupervised learning there is no y, only X. Specifically, an unsupervised algorithm does not predict anything. Instead, it aims to identify some kind of pattern or structure in the data. An example might be learning how to group customers into distinct segments that have similar requirements. In that case you have access to historical data about customer behavior (X) but no indication of what segments they should belong to. Instead, the unsupervised algorithm is tasked with coming up with customer segments using only the historical data provided. The output in this case is not a prediction, but a list of segments along with the customers that belong to each segment.

The distinction between supervised and unsupervised learning may seem clear-cut. In reality, some approaches combine elements of both (sometimes referred to as *semi-supervised learning*). Others, particularly some of the more recent approaches, do not fit clearly into either of these categories. I provide two examples: generative learning and reinforcement learning.

2.3   Generative learning

In *generative learning* the ML algorithm is tasked with creating something similar to what it was trained on, but not identical. An example would be a model that produced images of oil paintings similar to a set of training images of oil paintings. The key word here is *similar*. The algorithm is not expected to reproduce exact copies of examples in the training data, but novel images that nonetheless appear similar to those in the training set. Figure 2.1 presents a painting created by a generative learning algorithm. Another example closer to the world of business would be to generate plausible price histories of financial assets for risk management purposes. This could be used to augment limited real-world price data in conducting stress-tests.

2.4   Reinforcement learning

In *reinforcement learning* the objective of the algorithm is to learn a set of conditional behaviors (or *policy*) that brings it closer to a specified goal. A common example is game playing. In game such as chess the algorithm must be able to recommend a good next move for any possible legal board configuration. The difficulty is that it is often hard to tell whether a particular move is a good move at the time. Hence there is a need for the algorithm to identify good moves and reinforce those, while penalizing bad moves.

Figure 2.1 Generative algorithms – ML showing its artistic side
Source: Generated using the StyleGan2 ADA algorithm.

For instance, an electricity grid operator could use reinforcement learning to learn how to optimally deal with unexpected loads on the network in a way that keeps the power on while minimizing costs.

2.5   Online vs batch training

Another distinction is between online training and batch training. In *batch training* the algorithm is first trained on a "batch" of training data, and then deployed for use. In some cases it might be years before the algorithm is re-trained (if ever). In other cases the algorithm may be retrained far more frequently. *Recommender systems* which provide product recommendations to customers of online retailers may need to be re-trained monthly to learn from rapidly changing trends and behaviors. Nonetheless both are examples of batch training – training the model and deploying the model are separate steps.

In *online training* the algorithm learns from data continuously while in use. This is often needed in systems that control a process in real time. An example might be stability control for an off-road vehicle. The best way to manage stability control depends on the situation (snow, sand, mud and rock all have different implications for traction). In that setting the system can monitor whether its actions are having the desired effect, and if not, adapt in a direction that improves performance. Outside of real time systems batch training is the more common approach.

2.6   Value-destroying vs value-creating ML

There is a final distinction to make, and it is perhaps the most important one – value creating vs value destroying ML. Nothing guarantees that an ML solution will create value.

Not all problems are amenable to ML solutions. Helping you understand which problems are suitable candidates for solving with ML is one of the objectives of this book. Even when the problem can be tackled with ML, the quality of the implementation matters. In applications such as high-frequency trading a sub-par ML algorithm can lose millions of dollars before you have taken your next breath.

Sometimes the most value destroying ML solution is the one you *should have* built, but did not. Conversely, substantial value can be created by deploying ML solutions, particularly if you can do so ahead of competitors. The key point is that ML does not just create value in and of itself. Instead, you must first identify a problem *worth* solving.

The purpose of this book is to show you how to create ML solutions that add value rather than destroy it. This requires both technical and organizational skills – Part I of the book covers the former while Part II covers the latter.

Note

1   Be aware that the term "regression" means different things in statistics and machine learning. In statistics regression usually means estimating some kind of linear model. In machine learning, a regression task includes any approach that predicts a continuously valued number. So in machine learning a decision tree can be used for a regression task, but in statistics a decision tree would be considered an example of non-parametric methods (and not a regression). Conversely, a logit regression in statistics is used to predict a binary class. In machine learning a logit regression solves a classification task (despite containing "regression" in its name!).

3 Creating ML models

In this chapter we discuss the general approach taken when creating new ML models. Creating an ML model involves several distinct stages. While these stages are often presented sequentially (see Table 3.1), the reality is that there is a lot of back and forth when you actually do it. Creating an ML system is an iterative rather than sequential process.

3.1 Data, instances and features

Let's start by clarifying some terminology around data. The table below presents tabular data of the kind that might be encountered in a payroll system. Each row relates to a particular employee. These rows are referred to *instances* in ML, *observations* in statistics and *records* in database systems. Each column contains specific types of information that are recorded for each instance. These columns are referred to as *features* in ML, *variables* in statistics and *fields* in database systems. So Bob, Alice, Eve, Dan and Trudy are instances and ID, Name, Department, Seniority, Tenure and Compensation are features. It is conventional to present a data set with the instances in rows and the features in columns, just as one would present the data in a spreadsheet. The table as a whole is referred to as a *data set* in ML, a *sample* in statistics and a *table* in database systems.

Note that the features themselves are of distinct *types*. Tenure and Compensation are numbers that could vary more or less continuously within some reasonable range; we refer to these as *numerical features* or *continuous features*. Predicting Compensation would be regression task. Seniority might be a number that can only take on fixed values 1, 2, 3, 4 and 5, with a higher number indicating a higher level of seniority. In that case, seniority

DOI: 10.4324/9781003330929-4

ID	Name	Department	Seniority	Tenure	Compensation
0001	Bob	Engineering	3	5	160,000
0002	Alice	Engineering	4	6	220,000
0003	Eve	HR	2	3	110,000
0004	Dan	Finance	3	4	140,000
0005	Trudy	Senior Management	5	12	450,000

is an *ordinal feature* – it is the order of the numbers that matter, rather than their magnitude. Department is a variable that can take on values from a restricted set of possibilities, but with no particular ranking or ordering among them. This is an example of a *categorical feature*. Predicting a categorical value would be an example of a *classification* task.

3.2   Targets and inputs

In supervised ML we split the data set *vertically* into a single target variable column and one or more input variables (consisting of some or all of the other columns). For instance, we might wish to build a model to predict compensation. In that case, the single Compensation column would constitute the target variable y, while we could combine the Department, Seniority and Tenure columns into the input variables X. (We would probably not use the ID or Name columns as features in our model, since this should not have any bearing on compensation – at least in theory.) Note that when we separate the target y from the inputs X we are splitting vertically on features.

3.3   Training, validation and test data sets

The other kind of splitting common in ML is a *horizontal* splitting of instances into distinct (non-overlapping) training, validation and test data sets. This is a crucial step in building reliable ML systems. Throughout this chapter we will emphasize the link between each of the steps and the data sets they are applied to.

The need to split data this way might strike some as strange. The problem, paradoxically, is that ML algorithms are very good at finding patterns. This applies to both real and imaginary patterns, such as might appear in any noisy data. The solution is to regulate the power of the ML system so that it is sufficient to capture most of the real patterns but not so much that it starts fitting to random noise in the data. In other words, we are looking for a kind of "Goldilocks" power-setting such that the ML algorithm is neither too weak nor too strong. When too weak, the ML algorithm does not have enough power to capture even the real patterns in the data – this is known as *under-fitting*. When the ML algorithm has too much power it fits both real patterns and random noise with equal abandon – this is known as *over-fitting*.

If this discussion seems overly abstract, consider the example in Figure 3.1. We use made-up data created by adding random noise to an underlying signal represented by the dashed line. The made-up data points themselves are represented by circles. The deviations of the circles from the dashed line are due to random noise – we know since we created the data that way. (The benefit of using made-up data is that we *know* what is signal and what is noise. This is not generally true for real-world data.)

For prediction we rely on an ML approach known as *k-Nearest Neighbors* (kNN). The kNN algorithm is simplicity itself – when required to make a prediction, it looks for the *k* instances in the training data that are "closest" and use the average target variables of those instances as its prediction.[1] Consider what happens if we select *k* = 1. If asked to make a prediction for a training data instance, it will simply look for the closest instance in the training data (which will be itself!) and present that as the prediction. As a result, when predicting the target value of an instance located inside the training data it will never make a mistake. The algorithm will have effectively "memorized" the entire training data set, including both real patterns and

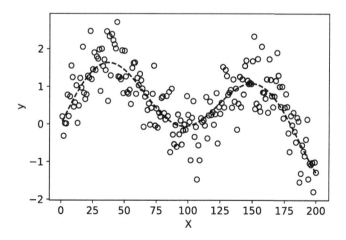

Figure 3.1 Synthetic data with signal and noise

any noise that happens to be in the training data. (In Figure 3.1 the dashed line is the true signal while the deviations of the circles from that line is due to the noise we added on purpose.)

If we relied on the training set performance (the dashed line with empty circles in Figure 3.2) we would have selected $k = 1$. With $k = 1$ the algorithm does not just do well on training data; it makes no mistakes whatsoever (the error rate is zero!). The problem is that when you present the algorithm with *validation* data that is not part of the training set it, performs poorly. The performance on the validation data is indicated by the solid line with solid dots in Figure 3.2. In ML, we are always interested in how the model performs on new, unseen data. (Otherwise you can simply look up the answer from historical data; that is at best a database problem, not an ML problem.) It follows that you should evaluate a model on data other than the data it was trained on; we call this either validation data (used for making choices during model development) or test data (for obtaining an unbiased estimate of the real ability of the trained model to handle new, unseen data). On validation data (the solid black line) the best performance is obtained with seven neighbors ($k = 7$), as indicated by the gray vertical line in Figure 3.2. (Admittedly, other choices of k in the range 4–16 yields similar performance in validation data, but $k = 7$ is the best overall, so we'll go with that.) This is an example of *hyper-parameter tuning*; selecting the best choice among

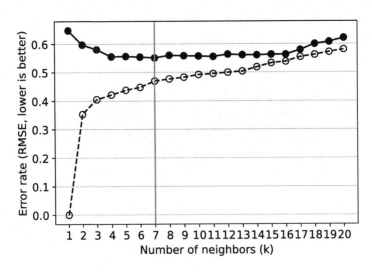

Figure 3.2 Hyper-parameter tuning with *k*-Nearest Neighbors

several different choices based on the performance of the algorithm on the validation data set.

Overfitting and underfitting are both detrimental to model performance as illustrated in Figure 3.3. The graphs in the first row illustrate overfitting using $k = 1$ neighbors. The left-hand graph shows the performance of the trained model on training data. The predictions (crosses) match the actual data points (circles) exactly. The right-hand graph shows the performance of the same trained model on validation data. When applied to validation data, the performance is far worse; the predictions no longer match the actual data closely. With $k = 1$ the predictions oscillate wildly around the "true" pattern indicated by the dashed line – the model overfitted.

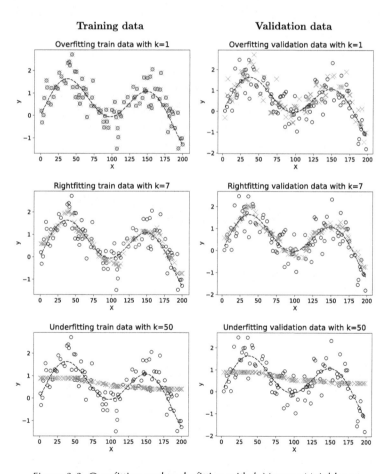

Figure 3.3 Overfitting and underfitting with k-Nearest Neighbors

The second row in Figure 3.3 shows the performance of a model trained using $k = 7$ neighbors, chosen because it yields the best performance in validation data. The accuracy is worse for training data (left-hand graph) but much improved for validation data (right-hand graph). Using $k = 7$ neighbors results in a trained model predictions (crosses) that tracks the "true" model (dashed line) fairly closely for both training data and validation data. The model is sufficiently powerful to fit most of the true pattern in the raw data without fitting too much of the noise.

The last row in Figure 3.3 shows the performance of a model where we use $k = 50$ neighbors. This results in a model that is far too constrained, yielding an almost straight line of predictions (crosses) that completely fails to fit the underlying pattern in the data (dashed line). In other words, the model is so weak that it fits neither the true pattern in the raw data nor the noise in the data.

Keep in mind that in this example we generated the data ourselves, so we can compare our model predictions against this "true" pattern. Using such made-up *synthetic data* is a common technique for exploring and trouble-shooting ML models. In real-world data we typically don't know what the true pattern is; that is why we use ML in the first place. Even so, selecting good hyper-parameters using validation data can help us create models that does not overfit or underfit too much.

3.4   The machine learning recipe

With this important discussion behind us, we turn to the steps typically involved in creating an ML system. Table 3.1 specifies 15 steps. Let's take them in turn.

3.4.1   Specify the problem

What is it – exactly – that you want the ML system to do? Why? How will you measure the performance of the system? How will the performance of the system translate into tangible benefits for your organization? What is the minimum performance needed for a viable system? Who will be responsible for creating the system? What is the expected cost and time to completion? (*Hint*: estimate the best case and the worst case. Double the worst-case estimate. That is your number.) It is a good idea to summarize the answers to these questions in a written document – that way everyone involved is on the same page, so to speak.

3.4.2 Collect the data

The kind of data you collect will obviously depend on the problem you are trying to solve. More importantly, the quantity, quality, variety and relevance of the data you can source will fundamentally determine the upper limit of what you can achieve with ML. Unless you already have the data sorted out, the data engineering aspect of ML is where you should spend most of your time and effort. This includes automating the acquisition and cleaning of data, establishing data dictionaries that describe the data and implementing privacy controls for sensitive data.

3.4.3 Split the data

You need to split the available data into three non-overlapping subsets, namely training data, validation data and test data. (See the discussion at the start of this chapter). To emphasize this Table 3.1 specifically indicates which of the data sets are involved in each step.

Before training a model there are usually several choices to make in terms of how you process the data and what settings (e.g. "dials and switches") you will use for the algorithm. We refer to these choices collectively as *hyper-parameters*. The *validation data* is used to evaluate the effect of different choices (hyper-parameters) on the performance of the ML system. The reason we use separate validation data is that we care about how well the trained model will do on *new, unseen* data. That is why we can't use the training data to evaluate the impact of different hyper-parameters. You cannot train a model until you have specified the hyper-parameters. (If you do not make any choices the ML algorithm will simply use its *default settings*, which are predetermined choices for each available setting. Not making a choice is still a choice!)

Algorithm + hyper-parameters → trainable_model (with hyper-parameters chosen by you based on validation data performance)

The *training data* will be used to estimate the parameters of your *trainable model*. (Recall that parameters refer to the internal "bits and pieces" that the ML algorithm fiddles with to improve its performance on the training data.) Once the parameters have been estimated on the training data the trainable model becomes a *trained model*, ready for use.

Table 3.1 The "recipe" for constructing a machine learning model

		Data splits			Artifact/
	Step	**Train**	**Validation**	**Test**	**output**
1.	Specify the problem				Problem statement
2.	Collect data	•	•	•	Data set
3.	Split the data	•	•	•	Split data
4.	Understand and explore the data	•	•		
5.	Preprocess the data, construct features	•	•	•	ML-ready data
6.	Select a machine learning approach				ML approach
7.	Select hyper-parameters (ML settings)				Trainable model
8.	Train the model	•			Trained model
9.	Evaluate the model on validation data		•		Performance measures
10.	If performance is weak go to 7 (6, ..., 1)				
11.	Else train the final model	•	(•)		Trained final model
12.	Evaluate the final model on test data			•	Performance measures
13.	If test performance is weak then:				
13a.	— Add the test data to train/validation	•	•		
13b.	— Get new test data			•	New data
13c.	— Go to 7 (6, ..., 1)				
14.	Else deploy the model in production				Production model
15.	Monitor the model				Performance measures

Trainable_model + training_data → trained_model (with parameters estimated from training data)

Once you have settled on the best hyper-parameters and trained your model, you need to evaluate it again on some new, unseen data. Neither the training data nor the validation data will do, since both were used in coming up with the trained model. That is why we have *test data* that is distinct from both the training data and the validation data. The performance of the trained model on the test data should provide a reasonable estimate of how the model will fare when it encounters new, unseen data (such as the test data).

ML methods generally assume that the same patterns hold in each of the training, validation and test data sets, that is to say they have the same *distribution*. When this is not the case, the ability of the ML algorithm to learn will decrease.

A common question is how much of the available data should be allocated to each of the data splits. The size of the validation and test data should be sufficient for calculating accurate performance metrics. The rest of the data can be used for training. For a small data set (hundreds of instances) a split of 60%/20%/20% might suffice for training, validation and test data sets. For very large data sets with billions of instances the split could be 98%/1%/1%. (If you have that much data, it might be worth keeping a few extra test data sets in your back pocket.)

In many contexts it is common to randomly allocate instances to each of the data splits. Random allocation also helps to ensure that the different splits have similar distributions (particularly if you have a lot of data). However, if you are looking to do *forecasting* you should split the data chronologically, since this mirrors what the algorithm needs to do in practice. When forecasting, you do not have the luxury of training on both past and future data – you can only train on past data.

3.4.4 Understand and explore the data

This is vital – you need to LOOK at your raw data (the actual numbers, not just graphs and summaries). Often this will reveal unexpected features or mistakes in the data. For example, in a financial data set, missing stock returns might be coded as -99. If you think this example is contrived – it isn't. *"In CRSPAccess, missing values were indicated by the use of defined non-null values (e.g -99 for returns and 0 for prices)."*; quoted from https://www.crsp.org/products/documentation/overview-4. Clearly you would not want your ML algorithm to treat this as a real stock return! It is common to report summary data for each variable (both target and features). The summary data typically includes the following statistics for each variable: mean, standard deviation, minimum, median, maximum and count of (non-missing) instances. (*Hint*: look for minimum and maximum values that doesn't make sense – for instance, age should not be negative, nor should it exceed 130 – at least for humans. Also look for variables with a standard deviation of zero. That means the variable is *exactly* the same for all instances; this is either a mistake, or merely a useless variable.)

Another useful way to look at the data is to calculate the correlations between different variables; this is usually reported in a square grid (*correlation matrix*) so you can look up the correlation between any two variables. Correlation measures how similar two variables are in the way they vary across the data set. The standard correlation measure ranges from −1 (completely opposite) to 1 (completely the same). A correlation of 0 means that there is no (linear) association between the two variables. Variables that are highly correlated (either very close to −1 or very close to 1) likely contain very similar information. Variables that are highly correlated with the target variable are particularly useful for prediction. When you explore the data, you should exclude the test data; this way you do not risk compromising the "never seen before" nature of the test data.

3.4.5 *Preprocess the data and construct features*

ML algorithms can be quite picky in terms of how data should be presented and structured. As a result, there is a need for preprocessing the data before feeding it to the ML algorithm. Common preprocessing steps include cleaning the data and fixing errors, merging disparate data sets into a single data set, filtering data, normalizing data,[2] reducing the number of features (*dimensionality reduction*), constructing additional features from existing data (*feature engineering*) and specifying variable types (numeric or categorical). Preprocessing steps and feature construction steps should be applied consistently but separately to each of the data splits (training, validation and test data). This is to avoid *data leakage*, which is when information from one data set finds its way into another.[3] We will discuss dimensionality reduction in Chapter 7.

3.4.6 *Select a machine learning approach*

Given the large array of ML algorithms, how should one pick the right one for a particular problem? There are a few rules of thumb.

The structure of the problem itself will generally rule out certain kinds of algorithms. If the problem requires predicting a number, that rules out classification algorithms. If instead you are looking to uncover structure in the data, that indicates an unsupervised learning problem, so neither regression nor classification approaches would be appropriate.

You should also look at the approaches used by other people to solve similar problems.

Once you have a few candidate approaches, you should try them out and pick the one that works best. (Caution: When "trying out" anything you should never refer to the test data. Use the validation data set for trying out things.)

3.4.7 Select hyper-parameters

Most ML algorithms have various settings ("dials and switches") that affect how they operate. Any setting that you intend to change to see if it improves performance becomes a hyper-parameter. (The others are merely potential hyper-parameters.) The same applies to any modeling choices you make by reference to how it affects the performance of the ML model, including choices regarding data preprocessing and feature engineering. So the machine learning approach you select based on how it affects model performance is properly speaking a hyper-parameter. Again, when making choices about hyper-parameters based on model performance, that performance should be evaluated on the validation data set (and *not* the training or the test data sets). Once you have specified your hyper-parameters you have a *trainable model* – one that is capable of being trained if provided with data, but not yet actually trained.

3.4.8 Train the model

Finally! This is usually straight-forward when using standard ML frameworks on reasonably sized data sets. It often involves little more that adding a `model.fit()` line to your code. On the other hand, when using novel, leading-edge algorithms applied to very large and complex data sets the training process itself can take weeks or months and millions of dollars of compute resources along with dozens of specialist engineers and scientists. Once the training process is complete, you have a *trained model*. Unlike a trainable model, a trained model is ready to make predictions from input data.

3.4.9 Evaluate the model on validation data

It is now time to see how the model performs on new, unseen data. We use the validation data set for this, as discussed at the start of the chapter. How should one evaluate the model? The exact kind of performance measure depend on the kind of algorithm. For regression problems RMSE (root mean squared error) and MAE (mean absolute error) might be used. In classification, measures such as accuracy and ROC-AUC (covered later) can be used. These measures attempt to quantify how well the ML model is doing in terms of predicting the target. If at all possible, one should also quantify the performance of the model in terms of its originally stated objectives. For instance, if predicting stock returns one should attempt to quantify the profitability of the resulting trading strategy, not only the error of the predictions. The hyper-parameter choices that minimize the prediction error are not necessarily the same as those that maximize trading strategy profitability; it is the latter that ultimately matters, not the former.

3.4.10   If validation performance is weak

Building ML models is an iterative process. As one proceeds through different stages, it is often necessary to revisit earlier stages as you learn things. If performance is not adequate, the priority should be to understand why. A closer examination of those instances where the algorithm makes mistakes can be very helpful. Sometimes the algorithm is right, and it is the *data* that is wrong. In that case fixing the data can make a big difference. A challenge is that if an ML algorithm is not working well, there are a great many things that might have gone wrong – the approach might not be a good fit for the problem, or the hyper-parameters may have been badly chosen, or maybe it is an error in the code, or perhaps an error in the data or even some combination of these issues. The standard problem-solving approach applies here. Come up with guesses about what the problem might be, fix them, and see if it helps. Some of these problems can be avoided by taking a deliberate, systematic approach to building the ML model. Start with a very simple model (so simple that it *can't* be wrong) and gradually add complexity in stages. We discuss this topic in more detail in Part II of the book.

3.4.11   Train the final model

By the time you reach this point, you may have trained the model hundreds or even thousands of times (in order to find and fix errors, tune hyper-parameters, etc.). How do you know when the candidate model is ready to be the final model? In an ideal world, it is when there is nothing left to improve. In reality, you stop when you run out of time, money or ideas. The output of this step is a *trained model*. It is ready to be applied to data, maybe even in the real world. But first you need to know if the model is any good, on new, unseen data. The performance on the training and validation data is no use. That data has already been "seen" by the model during training and hyper-parameter tuning. You need some really new, unseen data – the test data.

3.4.12   Evaluate the final model on the test data

That means measuring its performance on the test data. It is normal – indeed expected – for the performance on the test data to be weaker than on the validation data. However, it is the best estimate of what you should expect if the model is put into production. Again, if possible the performance of the model should also be quantified in terms of the original objective (reducing customer churn by x percentage, saving x dollars due to avoiding equipment failure, etc.). At this point stakeholders need to decide whether to proceed to deploying the model in production; or whether more work is needed. If the former, go to step 14, otherwise ...

3.4.13   If test performance is weak

If more work is needed, keep in mind that you no longer have untainted, pristine test data. You have taken a decision to change something (like the model or the data) based on the performance of the model on the test data, and as a result it is now longer new and unseen; that is, it is no longer truly test data. You will need to acquire new test data (the old test data can be allocated to the training and validation data sets). This does not present an issue if large amounts of new data are created naturally each day (online retailing platforms) or if data can easily be generated from experiments (like particle accelerators). But what should be done if there is no way to get more data? The only way a macro economist can get another 20 years of macro-economic data is to wait another 20 years (you can pull of this trick perhaps twice in your career). If you had enough data to begin with, this is the point where you realize it would have been a good idea to put aside a few more test data sets, just in case. But perhaps data was scarce even to begin with. In that case, you don't really have much choice but recycle your existing test data. Do be aware that from now on even the results on the test data are likely to over-state the true ability of the model.

It is important to understand that the problem is *not* that the test data is somehow corrupted or altered during the development process. The test data remains unchanged. The problem is that once you act to change the

model or approach by reference to test data performance, that test data is no longer qualifies as *unseen* data. But only performance on unseen data is a valid estimate of the performance of the model on unseen data! A useful analogy is exam questions, as we pointed out earlier in Chapter 1. If we wish to measure the true ability of students to solve problems of a particular kind, we present them with previously *unseen* questions of this kind in an exam. Once they have seen the exam questions, those questions can no longer be used to measure their true ability, only their ability to memorize answers. To again measure the true ability of students, we will need to come up with new, previously unseen, exam questions.

3.4.14 *Deploy the model in production*

This should be an easy step, but often isn't. The reason is that the trained ML model delivered in step 12 is often more in the nature of a proof-of-concept than a production-ready system. In fact, a whole new job description (ML Ops) has arisen to take stand-alone systems put together by data scientists and convert it into production hardened software that can make predictions at scale while allowing for redundancy, automated error reporting, links to other production systems for the supply of data and so forth. We'll have more to say about the realities of deploying systems in production in Part II of the book.

3.4.15 *Monitor the model*

Just because the model worked on the test set is no guarantee that it will continue to do so in production. Once in production, the environment may be different from the development environment and the quality of the data may not be the same. In short, things can break without any warning. For this reason it is imperative to monitor the model's performance in production continuously. It is also a good idea to have a "backup" model to fall back on if for some reason the newly installed ML model fails spectacularly on its first encounter with the real world (it has been known to happen). Even if nothing breaks or fails, it is common for the performance of ML models to deteriorate over time as the patterns in the real world evolve (this is known as *data drift*). As a result it might be necessary to re-train – or even re-engineer – the ML system from time to time.

The discussion in this chapter applies to most ML systems, and is in that sense quite general. To paraphrase Tolstoy, well-performing ML systems all work well in the same way, while problematic ML systems tend to be problematic in unique and confusing ways. Following the steps outlined in this chapter is no guarantee that you will end up with a well performing system – but it should improve the odds.

Notes

1   The distance between two instances can be calculated by treating the N features for each instance as a point in N-dimensional space and calculating the distance between them. The (Euclidean) distance between instance A located at $(a_1,\ldots,_N)$ and instance B located at $(b_1,\ldots,b_N)$ is given by $||A - B|| = \sqrt{(a_1 - b_1)^2 + \cdots + (a_N - b_N)^2}.$

2   To normalize a variable: for each variable, subtract the average value of the variable and then divide by its standard deviation. The resulting variables will all have a mean of zero and a standard deviation of one.

3   Data leakage can happen very easily if one is not careful. Consider what would happen if you scale some variable by its average level across the full data set. That variable now reflects information not only from the training data set, but also the validation and test data sets – data leakage! Hence it can no longer be used for training. This problem is avoided if the variable in each data split is scaled by the average level of that variable *in that particular data split*.

Linear models

In this chapter we will consider linear models. In a linear model the predicted target is equal to a weighted sum of the features plus an optional constant. If we have N features identified as x_1 through to x_N then a linear model to predict y would be written as:

$$y = a_0 + a_1x_1 + \cdots + a_Nx_N$$

In the above linear model a_0 through to a_N are the *model parameters* (also known as *coefficients* or *weights*) of the model. In fitting a model the goal is to choose parameters such that the predicted target variable corresponds as closely as possible to the actual target variable.

It is hard to overstate the ubiquity of linear models in empirical social science and medicine. If you pick up a random empirical journal article from psychology, political science, economics or finance, chances are that it will contain a table documenting the results of fitting one or more linear models. Linear models are popular in social sciences because it is easy to test hypotheses with linear models. Testing hypotheses – rather than maximizing predictive performance – is the bread-and-butter work of empirical social scientists.[1] By contrast in ML the focus is squarely on predictive performance.

4.1 A simple linear model

To introduce linear models I use a freely available data set of traffic volume on an interstate highway measured from 2012 to 2018.[2] Along with the hourly traffic volume, the data set also contains the time and date of the measurement along with a few other variables such as the state of the

DOI: 10.4324/9781003330929-5

Table 4.1 Ten instances from the traffic flow data set

Features (X)								Target (y)
Holiday	Temperature	Rain	Snow	Clouds	Date_time	Hour	Workday	Traffic_flow
0	289.36	0	0	75	2/10/2012 10:00	10	1	4,516
0	293.66	0	0	20	3/10/2012 18:00	18	1	4,623
0	287.1	0	0	1	3/10/2012 21:00	21	1	2,637
0	290.63	0	0	75	5/10/2012 0:00	0	1	627
0	280.15	0	0	90	5/10/2012 19:00	19	1	4,063
0	276.35	0	0	20	6/10/2012 5:00	5	0	688
0	271.23	0	0	20	8/10/2012 8:00	8	1	5,966
0	279.47	0	0	20	8/10/2012 11:00	11	1	4,411
0	282.94	0	0	40	8/10/2012 14:00	14	1	5,125
0	278.38	0	0	90	9/10/2012 8:00	8	1	5,765

weather and whether the particular day happened to be a public holiday or not. Unlike genomics or high-frequency trading, most people are familiar with traffic from their daily life. As a result, we are all *domain experts* knowledgeable about the process that generates traffic flow data. We show ten instances of the traffic data set in Table 4.1. The target variable which we want to predict is the traffic flow, or the number of vehicles that pass a specific location over the course of an hour.

Our first model assumes that there is a linear relationship between the volume of traffic and the hour of the day (measured from 0 to 23). In other words, we assume that traffic flow can be modeled as:

$$\text{Traffic\_flow} = a + b \cdot \text{Hour (model 1)}$$

In the equation above Traffic_flow is the target variable we wish to predict, while Hour is the single feature we will use to predict it with. We have two parameters – a is the *intercept* (also referred to as the *constant* or *bias*) while b is the *coefficient* or *slope* parameter.[3]

4.2   Training linear regression models

How do we determine the best parameters a and b? To answer this question, we need to be little more precise about what we mean by "best". The standard way to approach this question is to define a *loss function* (also known as *objective function*) that converts the actual and predicted target variables into a single number. By convention, loss functions are written so that smaller is better. While there are a great many potential loss functions, a very common approach is to minimize the sum of squared errors.[4] When applied to linear models, this is referred to as Ordinary Least Squares (or OLS). Most of empirical social science research depends on variations of OLS.

When we fit the simple traffic flow model, we obtain $a = 2,112$ and $b = 97$ so that the fitted (or trained) model can be represented as:

$$\text{Traffic\_flow} = 2,153 + 97 \cdot \text{Hour (fitted model 1)}$$

As it turns out, this is a spectacularly inadequate model. Figure 4.1 plots actual traffic volume against the daily hour (ranging from 0 to 23) as gray dots, while the predicted traffic volume is plotted as red crosses, on the validation data. (We don't show the performance on the training data, which is broadly similar. Following best practice, we don't look at test data results until our model is finalized and set in stone.)

Remember, *look at the data*. (Except the test data, of course!). Figure 4.1 shows that the relationship between traffic volume and the hour of the day is decidedly non-linear. As a result, our simple linear model struggles to fit the data. It may seem obvious, but for ML to work the model that you use must be able to model the data that you train on. This ability of a model to capture the salient patterns in the data is referred to as *representation* by

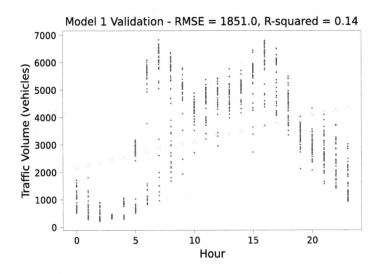

Figure 4.1 Traffic flow model 1 (validation data)

computer scientists. A model needs to be able to "represent" the patterns in the data (and hopefully not too much of the noise). In this particular case, our representation is flawed. The relationship between traffic volume and hour is not linear, and no amount of number crunching is going to remedy that shortcoming.

4.3 Using feature transformations in linear models

When a relationship is not linear, it is often possible to make it approximately linear using a suitable transformation of the features. This technique allows linear models to be used even if the features in the original data are non-linear. A cursory examination of Figure 4.1 reveals that traffic appears to peak around the early afternoon. A simple transformation would be to use the relative time difference between the current time and 13:00 (1 pm), that is RelHour = abs(Hour −13). This yields our second model:

$$\text{Traffic\_flow} = a + b \cdot \text{RelHour (model 2)}$$

When estimated on the training data, we obtain the following fitted model:

$$\text{Traffic\_flow} = 5,918 - 434 \times \text{RelHour (fitted model 2)}$$

Figure 4.2 shows the fit of our newly estimated model 2. The traffic flow is still plotted against the hour of the day, even though the model is specified in terms of the relative hours to 1 pm. This accounts for the "kink" at 13:00 hours. Visually, model 2 appears to be an improvement on model 1 – but how much of an improvement? To answer this question, we turn to *performance measures* that quantify how well the model performs. The graph titles in Figures 4.1 and 4.2 report two performance measures – RMSE and R-squared. Let's take them each in turn.

4.4 Performance measures for regression tasks

RMSE is an acronym for *Root Mean Squared Error*. To calculate it, you first subtract the predicted target from the actual target value to obtain the prediction error (this is the "Error" part). You then square these errors (the "Squared" part) and then take their average (the "Mean" part) before finally taking the square root (the "Root" part).[5] Squaring the errors effectively penalizes large errors more heavily than small errors. And since a squared error

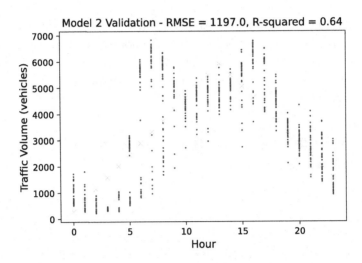

Figure 4.2 Traffic flow model 2 (validation data)

is always positive, it means that both positive and negative errors are penalized equally. The final square root means the RMSE measure is presented in the same units as the data. The model 1 validation data RMSE is 1,851 vs 1,197 for model 2, so model 2 is a meaningful improvement.

The *R-squared measure* tell us what fraction of the variation in the actual target value is explained by the model. It can be calculated as the square of the correlation between the actual and predicted target values.[6] In validation data model 1 explained only 14% of the variance in traffic flow while model 2 explains 64% of the variance in traffic flow, a very substantial improvement in explanatory power. (As an aside, these performance measures can be used in any regression task – it is not limited to linear models only. Classification tasks require their own set of performance measures, which we discuss in Section 6.3)

In summary, model 2 is a substantial improvement over model 1 – and all it needed was making a little tweak to the Hour feature.

4.5   Linear models with indicator variables and interactions

That said, we can do better. Closer inspection of Figure 4.2 reveals that the actual relationship between the hour of the day and traffic flow is not easily approximated by straight-line segments, despite the improvement in fit using model 2. We can address this by using hourly *indicator variables* (also known as *dummy variables*). That is, we introduce 23 new variables (H_1 to H_{23}) where H_n is equal to 1 for hour n only, otherwise it is set to zero.[7] Effectively we allow the model to take into account the empirical hourly pattern in the data rather than imposing our own linear pattern.

At this point our model would look like this:

$$\text{Traffic\_flow} = a + b_1 H_1 + \cdots + b_{23} H_{23}$$

Note that we no longer include an "Hour" variable, since the indicator variables (H_1 to H_{23}) now handles the modeling of the relationship between traffic flow and the hour of the day.

We can do more. If you squint a bit longer at Figure 4.2 you'll notice a curious pattern in the early hours of the day (6:00 – 9:00) and again in the mid-afternoon (16:00 – 17:00) where traffic flow is either high or low. This is where domain knowledge comes in handy. Those are the typical workday commuting patterns when people go to work and then return from work. What the data is telling us is that the pattern of traffic flow is different for weekdays (when there is a lot of traffic during peak times) and weekends and holidays (when people have more flexibility in terms of when and if they travel).

Let's introduce a "workday" indicator variable W set to 1 if it is a workday and zero if it is a weekend or holiday. In our case, simply including the workday indicator variable by itself won't help, because the difference in traffic flows depends on whether it is a workday *and* on the specific hour of the day. To handle this, we will make use of interaction terms. An *interaction term* is a new feature that you create by multiplying two individual features. The interaction term models the joint effect of the two original features that you multiplied together.

The revised model includes interactions between the workday indicator variable and each of the hour indicator variables:

$$\text{Traffic\_flow} = a_0 + a_1 W + b_1 H_1 + \cdots + b_{23} H_{23} + c_1 W\, H_1 + \cdots + c_{23} \times W\, H_{23}$$

This is getting just a little involved, so let's break it down. The intercept a_0 models the average level of traffic flow as well the level of traffic flow specific to hour 0 (the hour for which we did not include a dummy variable, also called the *base category*). The term $a_1 \times W$ models the average effect of it being a working day. The 23 terms $b_1 H_1$ through to $b_{23} H_{23}$ model the effect of each hour of the day independently. This what allows our model to handle arbitrary relationships between each hour of the day and the traffic flow. Finally, the additional 23 terms $c_1 W H_1$ through to $c_{23} W H_{23}$ handle the *incremental* impact of it being a workday on traffic flow for each of the hours. For instance, the estimated coefficient c_{12} will reflect the *additional* traffic flow we should expect to observe at 12:00 if it is a workday relative to a non-workday.

What else might affect traffic flow? Seasoned commuters will know that rainfall (or even worse, snowfall) can be the difference between being home in time for dinner and being home in time to go to bed. As luck would have it, our data set contains features for the temperature (Temp), rainfall over the past hour (Rain), snowfall over the past hour (Snow) and cloud cover (Clouds). Since each of these features might help fit the data we include them in the model. In doing so we impose a linear relationship between these additional weather variables and traffic flow.

The final model (model 3) looks like this:

$$
\begin{aligned}
\text{Traffic\_flow} = \ & a_0 \ [\text{the intercept term}] \\
& + a_1 W \ [\text{the workday indicator}] \\
& + b_1 H_1 + \cdots + b_{23} H_{23} \ [\text{the hourly indicators}] \\
& + c_1 W H_1 + \cdots + c_{23} W H_{23} \ [\text{workday} \times \text{hour}] \\
& + d_1 \text{Temp} \\
& + d_2 \text{Rain} \\
& + d_3 \text{Snow} \\
& + d_4 \text{Clouds}
\end{aligned}
$$

So, is all this work worth it? You bet! Figure 4.3 shows how well the model predictions match the empirical pattern of observations. The predictions follow the curves in the data (courtesy of the hourly indicator variables) and also appears to correctly anticipate different patterns of traffic depending on whether it is a workday or not (courtesy of the workday – hour interaction terms). The additional variation in the predictions reflect the impact of the weather-related features in the data. Model performance has also improved. In validation data the RMSE is now 507 (vs 1,197 for model 2). The R-squared measure has improved from 64% to 94%. This means that only 6% (100%–94%) of the variation in traffic flow is left unexplained by model 3.

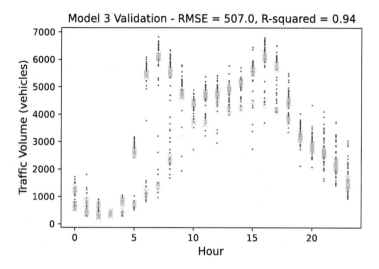

Figure 4.3 Traffic flow model 3 (validation data)

While one could always do more, this may be a prudent point to stop. (There is fine line between being clever and over-fitting the data). Since we have now committed to a final model, we are entitled to try it out on test data. Figure 4.4 shows that the performance on completely unseen data is a

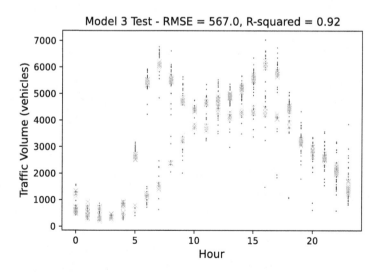

Figure 4.4 Traffic flow model 3 on test data

smidgen weaker, but still broadly in line with the performance we observed in the validation and training data. Success!

This is a good time to step back and summarize the benefits and drawbacks of linear models. The obvious constraint is that linear models can only fit, well, linear models. In practice, it may be possible to use a combination of well-chosen transformations, indicator variables and interactions to model data that, on the surface, appears to be non-linear and complex. Notice that it is you, the modeler, not the computer, that must choose these transformations, indicator variables and interactions. Therefore this will only tend to be a feasible approach in situations where the process generating the data is well understood and where the modeler has some experience working with linear models. The good news is that linear models are easy to understand and explain, at least when compared to other machine learning approaches.

If the process generating the data is complex, poorly understood, likely to be non-linear or potentially involves multi-way interactions, then linear models may not be the best choice. As we will show in the following chapters, ML methods built around neural networks or decision trees can automatically find and incorporate both non-linear effects and feature interactions. It is exactly the ability of those approaches to automatically accommodate non-linearities and interactions that make them so powerful.

4.6   Classification with logistic regression

The traffic flow forecasting problem is an example of a regression task; we need to predict a continuous number. What if we are facing a classification problem instead? Sticking with the traffic flow example, we might be interested in predicting whether a road is congested (1) or free flowing (0). One approach might be to use the existing traffic flow model and impose a cut-off for determining whether the traffic is free flowing or not. For instance, we could somewhat arbitrarily use a predicted traffic flow of 5,000 vehicles per hour as the cut-off – below this level we predict congestion and above this level we predict that traffic will be free flowing.

If the target variable is categorical (as it is in a classification task) then one can use a variant of linear models called *logistic regression*. Confusingly, logistic regression is only used for classification tasks and *not* regression tasks.

The reason for the confusing name is that in statistics regression means "linear model" while in ML regression means "prediction of a continuous number". Since the statisticians first invented logistic regression, their name stuck.

When using logistic regression the model is still linear, but rather than directly predict a number, the logistic regression model now predicts something called the log odds ratio, which can be converted into a number between 0 and 1 that reflects the probability of the road being congested. To generate the predicted class, one can use a probability threshold (normally 0.5) to convert the model probability into an actual forecast that is either 1 (if the probability is above 0.5) or 0 (otherwise). We'll discuss classification tasks in a bit more detail in Chapter 6.

4.7   Regularization – ridge regression, lasso and elastic net

Linear models often struggle if we use a large number of features (hundreds or thousands, rather than a dozen or so). In particular, linear models have trouble with features that are very similar (or highly correlated, to be exact).[8] When there are many features the likelihood that at least some of them are highly correlated increase rapidly. One solution is to only use a small number of variables that you are confident are at least somewhat independent – but this presumes a deep understanding of the data.

Note that most real-world variables have non-zero correlation with at least a few other variables. As long as each variable in the data exhibits meaningful variation that is independent of the variation in the other variables, it won't usually cause problems in linear models. It is particularly high correlation between features that causes problems. By way of example, in the last traffic flow model we included both Rain and Cloud features. Clearly, these are somewhat correlated, since there is usually some cloud cover when it is raining. On the other hand, it can also be cloudy when it is not raining. As a result the Rain and Cloud features are sufficiently different that including them both in the same linear model should not cause problems. On the other hand, rainfall measures from two locations a few hundred meters apart would essentially contain the same information, and including them both in a linear model would not be advisable.

In the presence of a large number of features *regularization* can be useful. Regularization is best understood as a collection of techniques that constrains the power of a model to reduce the risk of overfitting the data. The specific regularization techniques available depends on the ML approach being used. In the context of linear models, a common approach is to penalize "large" coefficients, thereby reducing the average magnitude of learned coefficients.

To constrain the magnitude of coefficients the usual least squares loss function is augmented by adding an additional *penalty term*. There are two common ways to calculate penalties in terms of the model coefficients. The first is the sum of absolute values of the coefficients (also known as the *L1 norm* or *L1 penalty*). The second is the sum of squared coefficients (also known as the *L2 norm* or *L2 penalty*). When penalty terms are used the algorithm attempts minimize both the sum of squared errors (as in normal OLS) *and* the penalty term (thus constraining the magnitude of the coefficients). The penalty term is typically multiplied by a hyper-parameter to regulate how much regularization should be imposed.

In *ridge regression* the penalty term is the sum of squared coefficients (L2 norm). Like OLS, ridge regression has a closed-form solution for calculating coefficients, which means it is cheap to compute.[9] *Lasso* uses the sum of absolute coefficients (the L1 norm) as the penalty term. Unlike ridge regression, there is no closed form solution for lasso, so in practice coefficients are determined using a numerical algorithm. One benefit of lasso is that it will often set coefficients exactly to zero – this is equivalent to omitting the corresponding features from the model. As a result lasso can be used for *feature selection*, that is, identifying the most promising features for use in a model.

In summary, linear models are well-suited to problems where the process generating the data is well understood and the relationship between the target variable and the features is approximately linear (or can be made approximately linear). In addition, linear models are easy to understand and explain. For this reason, it is not a bad idea to use a linear model as a "first cut", even if you know that the ultimate model might require something more powerful. On the other hand, much real-world data is generated by processes that are so complex that they are unlikely to be well represented by simple linear relationships. In those cases we need more powerful approaches such as the neural networks we describe in the next chapter.

Notes

1   The sheer variety of approaches and analytical firepower statisticians bring to hypothesis testing is awe-inspiring. See https://www.stata.com/features/ for an example of the approaches available in a modern statistics package.

2   The traffic flow data set is sourced from the UCI (University of California, Irvine) machine learning repository. The analysis presented in this chapter is based on a 10% random sub-sample of the data to reduce clutter in the graphs. See https://archive.ics.uci.edu/ml/datasets/Metro+Interstate+Traffic+Volume

3   One of the unwritten rules of statistical writing is that variables (such as targets and features) are represented by letters from the Roman alphabet (like x, y or z) while parameters to be estimated or learned from the data are represented by Greek letters such as α (alpha), β (beta), θ (theta) or γ (gamma). In my experience the use of Greek letters needlessly intimidate innocent people, which is why I avoid it in this book. For the record, in the machine learning literature θ or Θ (lower case and upper case Greek letter theta) is commonly used to represent the parameters of machine learning methods. In statistics it is common to use α (alpha) for the intercept and β (beta) for coefficients in linear models.

4   The least squares loss function is defined as follows: consider N instances indexed by i. Define the error of instance i as $\varepsilon_i := y_i - \widehat{y}_i$ (the difference between the actual target y and the predicted target $\widehat{y}$). The least squares loss function is then $L(\varepsilon) = \sum_{i=1}^{N} \varepsilon_i^2 = \varepsilon_1^2 + \varepsilon_2^2 + \cdots \varepsilon_N^2$. The least squares loss function is just the sum of squared errors.

5   In mathematical terms $\text{RMSE}(y, \widehat{y}) = \sqrt{\frac{1}{N} \sum_{i=1}^{N} (y_i - \widehat{y}_i)^2}$

6   The correlation coefficient between y and $\widehat{y}$ is given by $\rho(y, \widehat{y}) = \sigma_{y, \widehat{y}} / \sigma_y \sigma_{\widehat{y}}$ where $\sigma_{y, \widehat{y}}$ is the covariance between y and $\widehat{y}$ and σ_y and $\sigma_{\widehat{y}}$ are the standard deviation of the actual and predicted target values, respectively. The R-squared measure is then simply $R^2(y, \widehat{y}) = \rho(y, \widehat{y})^2$.

7   There are 24 hours in a day. We only include 23 dummy variables to avoid a technical issue called *perfect multi-collinearity*. The reason for this is somewhat technical; search for the term "dummy variable trap" if you are curious. Suffice to say that if you have k potential categories that you wish to model as indicator variables, you should only include $k - 1$ of those indicator variables in a linear model. Roughly speaking the intercept term in the linear model already takes care of the omitted category, so if you include it again it causes problems.

8   The problem is referred to as *multi-collinearity* in the statistics literature. The multi-collinearity problem can also occur if any linear combination of features are highly correlated with a different feature; hence even careful inspection of a

correlation matrix may not reveal a potential multi-collinearity issue. One consequence of multi-collinearity, when it is present, is excessively large and off-setting coefficient estimates, which in turn yields fragile models that do badly out-of-sample.

9   The linear algebra formula for OLS coefficients is $\beta_{OLS} = \left(X^T X\right)^{-1}\left(X^T y\right)$ where X is the *design matrix* containing the features (including a feature that is always 1, for modeling the intercept) and y is a column matrix containing the target value. In X the rows represent instances and the columns represent individual features. For ridge regression the coefficients can be calculated as $\beta_{Ridge} = \left(X^T X + \lambda I\right)^{-1}\left(X^T y\right)$ where λ is a scalar value that regulates the degree of penalization and I is an identity matrix with the same dimensions as $X^T X$.

5   Neural networks

If you read about yet another astounding advance in AI, chances are that it is powered by some variety of neural network. This is particularly true once we venture away from tabular data – such as might be found in a spreadsheet – and consider less-structured data such as sound, voice, images, video or natural language text. While originally inspired by models of the human brain, modern neural networks are best thought of as very powerful general purpose statistical approximation machines. (A theoretical result – the "Universal Approximation Theorem" – states that a neural network with at least two layers can represent any continuous function to an arbitrary degree of accuracy. At least in theory, if not always in practice.)

As always, this power comes at a cost. Large-scale neural networks require substantial computational power to train, and their very complexity makes it challenging to understand or explain how they do what they do. Nonetheless, neural networks have become the corner stone of modern ML.

5.1   A brief history of neural networks

Neural networks go by many names. In 1943 McCulloch and Pitts designed a single-layer neural network classifier that they called a *perceptron*. Later it was found that single-layer neural networks suffer from certain limitations which are alleviated if multiple layers are used. This led to *multi-layer perceptrons,* now better known as *neural networks* (or sometimes *artificial neural networks* or ANN's). Neural networks at that point were working well-enough that its eventual basis for AI were assumed in popular culture. For instance, in *Terminator 2: Judgment Day* the T-800 terminator played by Arnold Schwarzenegger explains *"My CPU is a neural-net processor; a*

DOI: 10.4324/9781003330929-6

learning computer. The more contact I have with humans, the more I learn". Some theoretical advances in the early 2000s allowed for the development of neural networks with many layers, which became known as *deep learning*. In 2018 Yoshua Bengio, Geoffrey Hinton and Yann LeCun were awarded the Turing Award (also known as the "Noble Prize of Computer Science") for their contributions to the deep learning revolution.

5.2 A linear model *is* a neural net (a very simple one)

So, how does a neural network work? The good news is that you have already seen a neural network. It turns out a linear model *is* a neural network, albeit a very simple one. We'll start with a simple linear model and gradually develop it into a fully general *feed-forward neural network* – the most "vanilla" kind of neural network.

Consider the following simple linear model inspired by the traffic flow data discussed in Chapter 4.

$$\text{Traffic\_flow} = b + w_1 \text{RelHour} + w_2 \text{Temp} + w_3 \text{Rain}$$

Imagine we are concerned about the possibility of a negative traffic flow prediction; a crude solution would be to simply replace negative predictions with zero. This augmented model could be written as:

$$\text{Traffic\_flow} = \text{MAX}\left(0, \ b + w_1 \text{RelHour} + w_2 \text{Temp} + w_3 \text{Rain}\right) \qquad (5.1)$$

Let's look at the structure of the model above. First, we multiply each of the inputs (RelHour, Temp and Rain) with their corresponding estimated parameters (w_1, w_2 and w_3) and then we sum those products. We then add an intercept (or bias) term b. Finally, we use the MAX(0, ·) function to replace negative results with zero. Replacing negative results with zero is commonplace in neural network calculations, where it goes by the exalted title of *rectified linear unit* (or *ReLU* for short). Thus ReLU(x) = max(0, x) = if $x <$ 0 then 0 else x. These same operations can be represented schematically as in Figure 5.1.

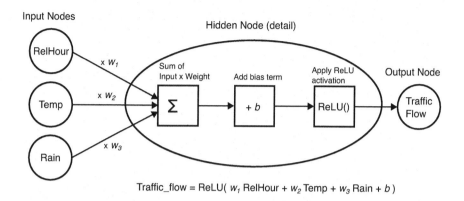

Traffic_flow = ReLU(w_1 RelHour + w_2 Temp + w_3 Rain + b)

Figure 5.1 A simple neural network (detail)

5.3 All you ever wanted to know about nodes

The neural network in Figure 5.1 calculates the same output as the linear model described in equation 5.1 above. In the neural network representation, inputs and outputs are represented as *nodes* (also known as *units* or *edges*). These nodes are drawn as circles or ellipses. The input nodes in Figure 5.1 are connected to a single hidden node via connections represented as arrows. The internal calculations of the hidden node is represented inside square boxes. (A *hidden node* is any node that is not an *input node* or an *output node*.) Each connection has a weight associated with it. You can image the input value traveling down the connection arrow and being multiplied by the weight as it does so. The receiving node sums all the inputs, where each input is the product of the value provided from the dispatching node and the weight associated with the connection itself (first box in the ellipse). It then adds a bias term to that sum (second box in the ellipse). Finally, an *activation function* is applied to the result (last box in the ellipse). In this example the activation function is ReLU(), which is commonly used today, but there are others such as sigmoid and tanh, which used to be more popular in earlier neural network architectures. It is the use of an activation function that allows a neural network to represent non-linear patterns.

The ellipse labeled "Hidden Node (detail)" in Figure 5.1 is in fact a single hidden node; we are just making explicit the calculation steps that take place in hidden node. The output of the hidden node is sent to the output node.

The output node does not apply an activation function. The connection between the hidden node and the output node also has a weight associated with it; to represent the linear model above we would simply fix that weight at 1 and the bias of the output node at zero. In that case the result generated by the hidden node is simply passed on to the output node. In general though, each connection has a weight associated with it and each *receiving* node has a bias associated with it, including the output node. In short, input nodes do not have bias terms or activation functions, hidden nodes have both bias terms and activation functions and output nodes have bias terms but no activation functions. Weights are associated with connections, not nodes.

The model in Figure 5.1 is a neural network that implements a linear model with the ReLU() activation function applied to the output. Let's introduce the term *activated linear model* to represent a linear model with an activation function applied to its output. We typically use a more compact representation for neural networks, where hidden nodes are represented by circles and the weights, biases and activation functions are not detailed. The first network in Figure 5.2a is a more compact representation of the neural network detailed in Figure 5.1; it contains three input nodes, a hidden node and an output node. It is understood that information travels from left to right; relative to a connection the dispatching node is on the left and the receiving node is on the right.

5.4 More complex neural networks

We are now ready to consider more complex neural network architectures that goes beyond what a linear model can represent. The second network in Figure 5.2b introduces a second node in the hidden layer. The output of this model is a linear combination of the two hidden nodes plus a bias term. The hidden nodes themselves are each activated linear models of the three input nodes. The activated linear model of the top hidden node and its input connections are rendered in bold.

This is the key insight: the value produced by each node in a neural network is an activated linear model with inputs drawn from all the nodes in the preceding (left-hand side) layer. This kind of neural network architecture is often referred to as a *feed-forward neural network*, since information travels forward from the input nodes on the left toward the output nodes on

(a)

(b)

(c)

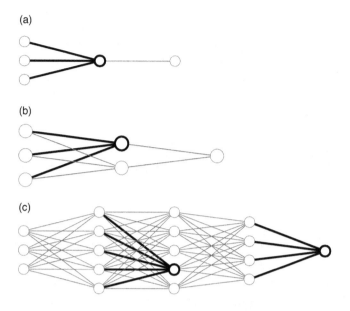

Figure 5.2 Neural networks. (a) One hidden layer containing one node, (b) one hidden layer containing two nodes, and (c) three hidden layers (five, five and four nodes respectively)

the right. The bottom network in Figure 5.2c is an example of a more realistic neural network with three hidden layers in addition to the three input nodes and the single output node. Each layer can have a different number of nodes; they do not need to be the same. To emphasize that neural networks are constructed by combining activated linear models, two of those activated linear models are rendered in bold in Figure 5.2c. A neural network will incorporate as many activated linear models as it has receiving nodes, or 5+5+4+1=15 in the case of the network in Figure 5.2c.

5.5   Training a neural network

How does a neural network learn? Simply put, it learns by finding values for the weight and bias parameters that yield good predictions. The weights and bias terms are the parameters of the neural network; the choice of neural network architecture (how many layers and how many nodes in each of them) is properly a hyper-parameter that should be determined by experimentation on the validation data.

51

Initially the weights and biases are set according to an *initialization scheme* which involves some randomness. At this point the performance of the neural network would no better than random guessing on average. The weights and biases are then updated through a training algorithm known as *back-propagation*. While the details are a bit involved, it can roughly be described as measuring the effect of a small change in each parameter on the performance of the model (as measured by the loss function)[1] and then making a small change to each parameter in the direction that would reduce the loss function.

This is an example of optimization by *gradient descent*. You could visualize this as descending the "loss function mountain" by traveling in the direction of the steepest downwards angle at each step. The loss function itself depends on the entire training data set. When the entire training set is used each time the parameters are updated, it is referred to as *batch gradient descent*. It is often more efficient to do the parameter updates more frequently using small blocks of the training data; this is known as *stochastic gradient descent*. Each time the entire data set is processed for training is called an *epoch*. It usually takes several tens to thousands of epochs to train a neural network, depending on the data and the type of problem.

Gradient descent works best if all the features have a similar scale; for this reason it is common to *normalize* features. One way to achieve this is by subtracting the feature average from each individual feature, and then dividing that number by the standard deviation of the feature.[2] Any scaling should be applied separately to the training, validation and test data sets to avoid data leakage.

One important consideration when training a neural network is the size of the adjustments made to parameters (or the length of the strides as you descend the loss function mountain). This parameter is referred to as the *learning rate*. If the learning rate is set too low, it will take a long time to train the model. This is a bit like climbing down a mountain one inch at a time. If the learning rate is set too high you may fail to reach the minimum loss or in extreme cases, make matters worse. This is a bit like taking strides measuring 10 miles – you are likely to step right past the lowest point and may actually end up higher than where you started from. The learning rate is yet another hyper-parameter that you can determine by experimenting on the validation data.

How long should you train a neural network? In other words, how many epochs of training is enough? As you may have guessed, this is also a hyper-parameter. But there is a useful trick called *early stopping* that allows us to pick the optimal training time with little additional effort. It works like this: at the conclusion of each epoch you measure the performance of the current model on the validation data. When the validation data performance no longer improves, you stop training the model. Early stopping is a useful technique to avoid overfitting the data, since you stop training the model as soon as it starts to overfit the training data based on evaluation against the validation data.

If you would like to see a neural network in action, you can head over to https://playground.tensorflow.org/ where there is a toy neural network you can play with. You can add layers, change the activation function and in general try out different things. It is a great way to build intuition about how a neural network works.

5.6 The MNIST example

Let's try our hand at a more realistic example – handwriting recognition. Figure 5.3 shows examples of handwritten numerical digits from MNIST, a well-known data set in ML. Each digit is a gray-scale 28-by-28 pixel image. Not all digits are well formed; I have circled those that, in my opinion, would not have met the standard at my primary school. Since Figure 5.3 contains 100 example images (10 examples for each of the 10 digits)

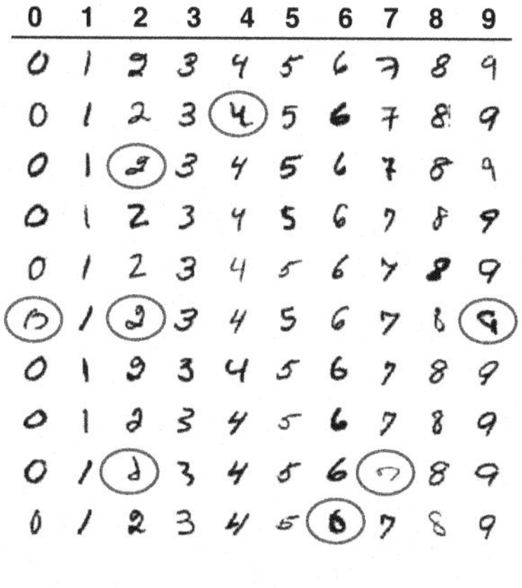

Figure 5.3 The MNIST handwritten digits

the 8 "malformed" examples account for around 8% of the data set with the remaining 92% unlikely to trouble a human reader. Thus to be worthwhile a machine learning solution should achieve an accuracy of at least 92% or better. As we will see a simple feed-forward neural network with two hidden layers can achieve an accuracy of around 97%.

The code to achieve this performance leverages the Keras interface that is now part of the Tensorflow ML library maintained by Google.[3] Since it is sometimes instructive to "peek under the hood" I present a code snippet that defines the neural network in Figure 5.4. Lines 5–9 import various ML elements needed to build the neural network. Lines 12–16 defines the architecture of the neural network. The neural network is based on the `Sequential` model, which simply implements a feed-forward design where the output from each layer is passed sequentially to the next layer. On line 13 the `Flatten` "layer" is really just a preprocessing step that flattens the 28×28 images into a linear array of 784 elements. Hence the input layer of the neural network consists of 784 input nodes with each representing an individual pixel in the digit image. This is followed by a single `Dense` hidden layer with 128 nodes and ReLU activation (line 14). (The `Dense` nomenclature simply refers to the fact that each node in the layer is "densely" connected to every node in the preceding layer.) The output layer, which is also densely connected, consists of ten nodes and a softmax activation. Why do we have ten output nodes instead of one? The reason is that this particular problem is a classification task. The model is required to classify each image into one of the ten possible categories corresponding to the digits 0–9. The softmax activation function ensures that the sum of all the output nodes adds up to 1.[4] Hence the value of output node i reflects the probability that the image is the digit i, where the output nodes are labeled from 0 to 9.

Lines 26–30 specify other elements of the neural network. The optimizer refers to the algorithm used to find the best network parameters; in this case it uses the Adam algorithm with a learning rate of 0.001 (line 20). Line 21 specifies the loss function. Since this is a classification task, the usual least squares loss function used for regression tasks is not appropriate. Instead, we specify a loss function that is specifically designed for multi-class classification, the *sparse categorical cross-entropy loss function*.[5] Line 22 specifies that a performance metric be reported. Effectively it reports the fraction of instances for which the neural network's best guess (highest probability) digit corresponds with the true digit – in this case it corresponds exactly with what we normally think of as accuracy.

```
1  # Extracted from https://www.tensorflow.org/datasets/keras_example
2  # With minor changes
3
4  # import Keras elements from tensorflow
5  from tensorflow.keras.models import Sequential
6  from tensorflow.keras.layers import Flatten, Dense
7  from tensorflow.keras.optimizers import Adam
8  from tensorflow.keras.losses import SparseCategoricalCrossentropy
9  from tensorflow.keras.metrics import SparseCategoricalAccuracy
10
11 # Define neural network architecture
12 model = Sequential ([
13    Flatten(input_shape=(28, 28)),
14    Dense(128, activation="relu"),
15    Dense(10, activation="softmax")
16 ])
17
18 # Define loss , optimizer and metrics
19 model.compile (
20     optimizer = Adam(learning_rate=0.001) ,
21     loss=SparseCategoricalCrossentropy(),
22     metrics=[SparseCategoricalAccuracy()],
23 )
24
25 # Fit the model by training for 6 epochs
26 model. fit (
27     ds_train ,
28     epochs =6 ,
29     validation_data = ds_test ,
30 )
31
32 # train accuracy = 0.9819, test accuracy = 0.9746
```

Figure 5.4 Defining and training a neural network in Keras

The last few lines (26–30) specify that the model should be trained for 6 epochs on training data `ds_train` and validation data `ds_test`. (In this particular example there is no hyper-parameter tuning performed, so we only use training and test data sets.) The accuracy is 98.2% on training data and 97.5% on test data, which is likely competitive with human level performance on similar tasks.

5.7   A peek into the future – transformers and language models

To be perfectly frank, we are only scratching the surface of deep learning in this chapter.[6] Most cutting-edge systems use more specialized neural network architectures than the simple feed-forward neural networks described here. For image recognition a variant known as *convolutional neural networks* (CNN's) seems to work quite well. For tasks that involve sequences of unstructured data such as natural language an architecture known as *transformers* have recently become prominent.

Instead of writing a paragraph explaining transformers, I thought it might be instructive to ask GPT-3, a transformer-powered natural language model created by OpenAI, to do so instead.[7]

Prompt: Provide a technical explanation of how the transformer architecture uses attention to model natural language.

GPT-3 answer: *The transformer architecture uses attention to model natural language by allowing the model to focus on specific parts of the input sequence when making predictions. This means that the model can learn to selectively pay attention to certain parts of the input sequence that are more relevant for the task at hand, and ignore other parts that are less relevant. This allows the model to better learn the relationships between words and concepts in natural language, and ultimately improve the accuracy of its predictions.*

While we are at it, we might as well ask how the role of machine learning is likely to affect business and industry ...

Prompt: How will the adoption of machine learning affect business and industry in the future?

GPT-3 answer: *The adoption of machine learning will have a profound effect on business and industry in the future. Machine learning will enable businesses to automate many tasks that are currently performed by human employees. This will result in increased efficiency and productivity, as well as reduced costs. In addition, machine learning will enable businesses to make better decisions by providing them with more accurate and timely data.*

Hopefully these answers provide some indication of the power inherent in these large-scale transformer models! (Section 8.3 discusses transformers further in the context of unstructured data.) Next, we will consider tree-based ML approaches such gradient boosting machines; one of my personal favorites for building ML models that just work.

Notes

1   More precisely, the partial derivative of the loss function with respect to the parameter.

2   Or in math, normalized$(x) = \frac{x - \bar{x}}{\sigma_x}$

3   The Keras code can be found here: https://www.tensorflow.org/datasets/keras_example. Curious readers can execute the code on a cloud service hosted by Google by clicking on the "Run on Google Colab" button.

4   Softmax applied to $x_1, \ldots, x_N$ inputs yield outputs $z_1, \ldots, z_N$ where $z_i = e^{x_i} \left(\sum_{j=1}^{N} e^{x_j} \right)^{-1}$

5   The "Sparse" refers to a more efficient representation of the matrices used internally in the algorithm. Categorical cross-entropy loss for $K > 1$ classes and M instances is defined as $L_{CE}(y, \widehat{y}) = -\frac{1}{M} \sum_{m=1}^{M} \sum_{k=1}^{K} y_{m,k} ln(\widehat{y}_{m,k})$ where $y_{m,k}$ and $\widehat{y}_{m,k}$ refers to the actual and predicted target values respectively for class k in instance m.

6   "Deep Learning" by Goodfellow, Bengio and Courville is the indispensable textbook covering deep learning. It can be accessed online at https://www.deeplearningbook.org/

7   The GPT-3 family of transformer language models can be accessed at https://beta.openai.com/playground.

6 Tree-based approaches, ensembles and boosting

When operating with tabular data, tree-based methods occupy the ML sweet-spot in terms of power and interpretability. Tree-based models are much easier to interpret and explain than neural networks and, when combined in boosted ensembles, are far more powerful and flexible than linear models (and often even neural networks).

6.1 The Titanic example

Let's illustrate tree-based prediction with a historical event – the sinking of the Titanic in 1912. Of the more than 2,000 passengers and crew only around 700 survived. Now imagine we were interested in predicting whether someone would have survived the event based on a small number of features such as age, sex and passenger class. At this point one could advance various theories as to which personal attributes might have aided in survival. Taking an optimistic view of human nature, let's say we subscribe to the "women and children first" ethos of that age. To make our model concrete we construct a flow chart which provides the predicted outcome, as in Figure 6.1. This is an example of what is called a *normative model*; a model of how the world *should* work, rather than how it *does* work.

It should not come as a surprise to readers that the world often does not work the way we would like it to. Examining the world as it is, rather

DOI: 10.4324/9781003330929-7

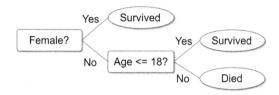

Figure 6.1 Manually constructed Titanic survival decision tree

than as we would like it to be, is the domain of *empirical* or *descriptive models*. On the normative vs descriptive scale, ML is situated very much on the descriptive side. Most ML models are atheoretical; depending on the problem, this may be a benefit or a drawback. ML works backwards from the data to come up with a model that explains the data. Models that are inspired by theory are usually constructed first, and only then tested to see if it corresponds with what we see in the real world.

In the context of predicting whether someone would have survived the Titanic disaster, ML tries to find a *decision tree* that best fits the actual data. It does so by "growing" the decision tree one rule at a time, at each point picking the rule that improves the predictions the most. Figure 6.2 shows the tree constructed on a training data subset of Titanic passenger records. Let's consider the topmost box; it tells us that there are 1,047 instances in the

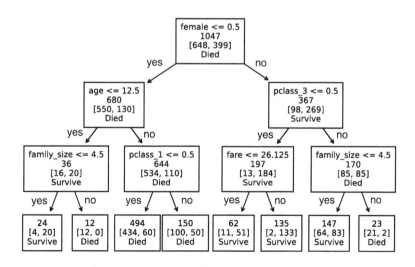

Figure 6.2 Machine learned Titanic survival decision tree

training data (second line in the box), 648 which are classified as "Survive" and 399 that as classified as "Died" (third line in the box). It therefore concludes that the most likely outcome for a passenger we know nothing about will be that they died (last line in the box). The first line in the box contains the first rule: "female $\leq$ 0.5". This requires a little unpacking; female is an indicator variable set to 1 if the passenger was female and 0 otherwise. So the rule is really stating "Not female", since female $\leq$ 0.5 is false if female = 1.

Interestingly, the tree-learned model concurs with our intuition regarding the importance of gender; no other variable is better at distinguishing between survival and death than asking whether the passenger was female. What happens next is that the training data set is split in two depending on whether the rule in the box is true (yes) or false (no). If the rule is true, it means that female = 0, hence male. For male passengers, the best prediction of survival is age. Young male children (age $\leq$ 12.5) had a much better chance of survival (20/36= 56%) than older children and men (110/644=17%).

For females the best predictor of survival is not age, but rather whether they traveled in first or second class (right-hand box below the top box, with rule "pclass_3 $\leq$ 0.5"). There were three passenger classes: first, second and third. We model these using indicator variables in the data (unlike linear models there is no need to omit one of the classes when using tree-based methods). The indicator variable pclass_3 is equal to 1 if the passenger traveled in third class and 0 otherwise. Hence the rule "pclass_3 $\leq$ 0.5" can be read as "not third class". Female passengers traveling in third class had a much lower chance of survival (85/170=50%) than those traveling in first or second class (184/197=93%), but similar to that of male child under 16 years of age (56%).

This discussion covered the first three rules which partitioned the training data into four groups corresponding to the four boxes in the second to last row of Figure 6.2. Each of those groups can be split yet again to yield a total of 8 possible outcomes (the last row of boxes in Figure 6.2). Those boxes at the end of the tree (predictably called *leaf nodes*) are where the predictions are made.

In a classification problem, such as the Titanic example we covered, the prediction for instances allocated to a leaf node is simply the training data class that forms the majority in that leaf. Let's consider the left-most box at the bottom of Figure 6.2 (the first leaf node from the left). This leaf node contains instances (i.e. passengers) that passed the tree rules from the top of the decision tree to the leaf node. This means that this leaf node contains passengers that were female (female ≤ 0.5), aged below 12.5 years (age ≤ 12.5) and belonged to a family of fewer than 5 (family_size ≤ 4.5). The 24 passengers in the training data that fit that description are all allocated to the leftmost leaf node. Of them, 4 died while 20 survived, giving a survival probability of 20/24=83%, which is much better than the average survival rate in the training data of 399/1,047=38%.

6.2   Making predictions with a tree model

So how do we use a trained decision tree such as the one in Figure 6.2 to make predictions on *new* data? For a new instance, we simply traverse the decision tree by following the rules at each step until we reach a leaf node. The prediction is then simply the class in that leaf node with the highest number of training data instances. Try it yourself. What is the predicted outcome for a 67-year-old male passenger that paid a fare of 45 pounds for a first-class ticket?[1]

Decision trees can also be used for regression problems; the tree construction works the same way. The only difference is that when we reach a leaf node the prediction is calculated as the average of the target value of training data instances that were allocated to that leaf node.[2]

By branching repeatedly on the same variable, a tree can approximate any non-linear patterns in the data. Trees can also represent variable interactions by branching on different variables along the way to the leaf node. This ability to automatically represent non-linearities and interactions in the data is a major strength of tree predictors relative to linear predictors. As we saw in Chapter 4, linear models can be specified in a way that can accommodate non-linearities and interactions. However, in linear models this is a manual process that requires both manual effort and a deep understanding of the data generating process. With trees non-linearities and interactions are automatically accommodated without requiring manual intervention or deep domain expertise.

Another benefit of trees is that it is robust to *order-preserving transformations* of the features. An order-preserving transformation is a transformation applied to a feature such that sorting on the transformed feature yields the same order as sorting on the original feature. In practical terms, consider some feature that is always positive, such as age. A tree using age as an input will make exactly the same predictions if you use age in years, or months or days, or if you add or subtract the same number to age, or if you take the logarithm of age, or the square, or the square root, or even $\frac{1}{9}\sqrt{ln((age + 3.1415)^5))} + 77$ (whatever that might mean ...).[3] It is only the relative ranking of features that matter when training tree predictors, not the actual numbers. This makes trees particularly robust to the various idiosyncrasies that crop up in real-world data.

6.3 Performance measures for classification tasks

We discussed performance measures earlier in the context of regression tasks (see Section 4.4). Classification models require a different set of performance measures, since the output of a classifier is not a continuous number, but rather a specific class. As a result common regression performance measures such as RMSE is not even well-defined for classification models.

6.3.1 Confusion matrices

The usual starting point for evaluating the performance of a classifier is to construct a *confusion matrix*. A confusion matrix is a two-way tabulation of the actual outcome and the predicted outcome from a particular classifier. Table 6.1 presents a generic confusion matrix (Panel A) and a confusion matrix based on the Titanic predictions using the tree model on test data (Panel B).

Table 6.1 Confusion matrices

A: A generic confusion matrix

		Predicted	
		Negative (0)	Positive (1)
Actual	Negative (0)	True Negative (**TN**)	False Positive (**FP**)
	Positive (1)	False Negative (**FN**)	True Positive (**TP**)

B: Confusion matrix for Titanic test data predictions (N=262)

		Predicted		
		Died (0)	Survived (1)	Total
Actual	Died (0)	**TN** = 139	**FP** = 26	165
	Survived (1)	**FN** = 22	**TP** = 75	97
	Total	161	101	**ALL**=262

By convention the actual true outcome is contained in rows, while the predicted outcome is contained in columns. The four cells in the confusion matrix reflects all the different ways in which a classifier can succeed or fail. Let's start with the upper left cell – *true negatives* or TN. True negatives are a count of those instances where the model correctly predicted a negative outcome. (In confusion matrices "true" and "false" is synonymous with "correctly predicted" and "incorrectly predicted"; it refers to whether the model got it right or not.) In the Titanic example our model correctly predicted 139 of the 165 actual deaths. *False negatives* (FN) refer to incorrect model predictions of the negative class. We can see that our tree model incorrectly predicted the death of 22 people who in fact survived. *True positives* (TP) refer to instances where the model correctly predicted a positive outcome. In the Titanic example our tree model correctly predicted the survival of 75 people (bottom left cell in the confusion matrix). Finally, *false positives* (FP) refer to instances where the model incorrectly predicted a positive outcome when in actual fact the outcome was negative. In the Titanic example our model predicted survival for 26 people who in actual fact had not survived.

Confusion matrices are a great way to understand and troubleshoot the performance of a classification model. You might recall that in our very first code example (Figure 1.1 in Chapter 1) we found that our loan classification model "cheated" by simply classifying every loan as performant. In a confusion matrix, you would be able to detect this behavior straight away since the true negative cell would be zero, indicating that the model never correctly identifies a non-performant loan.

6.3.2 Classification performance measures

Several classification performance measures are based on confusion matrices. We'll discuss a few of the more common ones. Perhaps the most obvious performance measure is *accuracy*. For once, this means exactly what you think it does. Accuracy is simply the fraction of correct predictions made by the classification model, in other words the sum of true negatives and true positives, divided by the total number of instances.

$$\text{Accuracy} = \frac{\text{TN} + \text{TP}}{\text{ALL}}$$

In some situations it is really important that the model correctly predicts positive outcomes in particular. To make this concrete, consider an extreme example – a "robocop" that shoots out the tires of any vehicles it classifies as stolen. On the whole, most people would rather that robocop miss a few genuinely stolen vehicles as long as it never, ever shoots out the tires of a vehicle that is not, in fact, stolen. The relevant measure here is *precision*, the ratio of true positives to all actual positives.

$$\text{Precision} = \frac{TP}{TP + FP}$$

In our contrived robocop example, we would insist on a precision measure very close to 100%, if not exactly 100%. Note that maximizing precision is the same as minimizing FP – if there are zero FP, then precision is exactly 100%. Hence precision is the relevant measure if even a small fraction of FP predictions is intolerable.

Now consider a kinder, gentler robot (let's say "robowarden") that can also detect stolen vehicles. Unlike robocop, when robowarden detects a stolen vehicle, it uploads relevant details (time, location, license plates, video feeds, etc.) to a central control room staffed by law enforcement officers. In this case a false positive does not really matter too much – at most it might waste a minute or two of an officer's time. On the other hand, we would prefer that robowarden miss as few truly stolen vehicles as possible. In this case the relevant measure is *recall*; the ratio of actual positives that are correctly flagged as positive by the model.

$$\text{Recall} = \frac{TP}{TP + FN}$$

If recall is high, then it means very few vehicles that are actually stolen will escape reporting by robowarden.

As you might already suspect, in classification models we trade off precision for recall – we can usually improve one at the cost of the other. For instance, we could achieve a recall measure of 100% by simply classifying every instance as positive (much like the loan performance classification example from Chapter 1). On the other hand, we could achieve 100% precision by simply classifying a *single* instance as positive, as long as that instance is in fact positive.

6.3.3 Thresholds and the ROC-AUC measure

In many classification models it is possible to change the threshold the model uses internally to decide whether an instance is classified as positive or not. When the threshold is increased, precision will generally increase at the cost of recall. Conversely, when the threshold is lowered, recall will generally increase at the cost of precision. It is important to stress that all the numbers in the confusion matrix depends on a particular choice of threshold. When the threshold is changed, the confusion matrix will also change, and along with it any of the performance measures that depends on it, such as accuracy, precision and recall. With tree predictors we accomplish this by predicting the probability that an instance belongs to a class, rather than predicting the class outright. The outright predictions are then made by comparing the predicted probability against the threshold. This is illustrated in Figure 6.3. As the threshold (x-axis) is varied, the recall and precision measures (y-axis) change in response. In this particular example the "sweet spot" seems to be a threshold of around 0.2 which yields recall and precision measures in the range 85%–90%.

Clearly this complicates the evaluation of classification models. Since performance measures depend on the chosen threshold, how should one judge the overall performance of a classifier across all possible thresholds? The answer lies in the ponderously named Receiver Operating Curve - Area Under the Curve measure (usually called the ROC-AUC or just AUC). The Receiver Operating Curve (ROC curve) plots the *true positive*

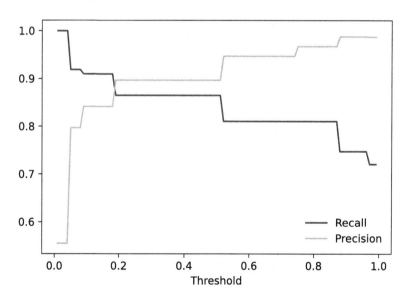

Figure 6.3 Recall and precision vs threshold
Note: Constructed from synthetic (made-up) data.

rate (TPR = TP/ALL) against the *false positive rate* (FPR = FP/ALL) across a range of different thresholds (Figure 6.4). To get a sense of what this curve means, consider the best possible model. Such a model would have a TPR of 100% and a FPR of 0%. In short, it would never make a mistake of any kind. The Receiver Operating Curve of such a perfect classifier would consist of a vertical line up from FPR=0, connected to a horizontal line going right at TPR=1, as indicated by the green line in Figure 6.4. A classifier that had zero skill, equivalent to just randomly guessing the class, would approximate a diagonal line from 0,0 to 1,1, as indicated by the diagonal line.

Most real-word classifiers fit between these extremes, as indicated by the tree classifier (the curved blue line in Figure 6.4). These curves can be summarized in a single performance metric, called ROC-AUC. The AUC part stands for "Area Under the Curve" and that is exactly what it is. A perfect classifier has a ROC-AUC of 100% while random guessing will yield around 50% on average. The ROC-AUC of the tree classifier is slightly above 90% on the synthetic data used in Figure 6.4. What constitutes a "good" score really depends on the difficulty of the classification task. For some tasks a ROC-AUC of 70% might be excellent performance, while for others that would hardly rate as trying. Performance measures are most meaningful when used to compare different models.

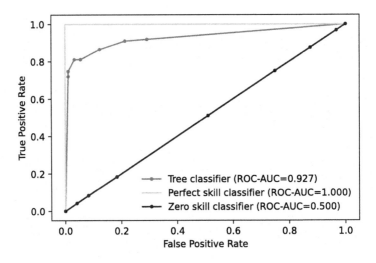

Figure 6.4 The receiver operating curve (ROC)
Note: Constructed from synthetic (made-up) data.

After this rather detailed discussion, it might come as a disappointment to learn that tree predictors have their own drawbacks. In particular, trees predictors are prone to overfit the data if grown too deep. On the other hand, if not grown deep enough, tree predictors may fail to model some of the more nuanced patterns in the data. Fortunately, there are approaches that mitigates these issues – ensembles of trees such as random forests and gradient boosting trees.

6.4   Ensembles and random forests

An *ensemble* is an ML model that is itself constructed by combining two or more subsidiary ML models, in much the same way that a large corporate enterprise might consists of dozens of smaller subsidiaries.

In ML we face a trade-off between *bias* (a measure of accuracy) and *variance* (a measure of how well the model generalizes to new data).[4] Increasing the power of a model tends to reduce bias but at the cost of increasing variance and *vice versa*. The power of ensembles derives from their ability to reduce variance while maintaining a similar average bias. In the same way that a diversified portfolio of financial assets can reduce overall risk, an ensemble of diversified predictors can reduce variance without significantly increasing bias. In short, ensembles allow us to make better bias/variance trade-offs than if we relied only on a single model.

In practice it is unusual to see ensemble models consisting of wildly disparate subsidiary ML approaches. (One exception is online ML competitions, such as those hosted by Kaggle,[5] where every last fraction of performance counts and model complexity be dammed.)

Random forests are a good example of the ensemble approach. A *random forest* consists of many individual tree predictors, each trained on a random subset of the available training data. The prediction from a random forest is simply the average prediction of all the individual trees contained in the random forest. The bias of the individual tree predictors is similar on average. However, since they were trained on different subsets of training data, their predictions are all somewhat different. By averaging across all the trees predictions the overall variance is reduced while maintaining a similar average bias. This reduction in variance can be "traded" for a reduction in bias by slightly increasing the power of the tree predictors (perhaps by increasing the allowable depth of the trees).

6.5   Gradient boosting machines

Random forests used to be a state-of-the-art ML approach, and it remains a popular approach today. However in the most demanding applications random forests have been largely superseded by gradient boosting machines.

Gradient boosting machines (GBMs, also known as gradient boosting trees or boosted trees) and random forests are both ensembles of tree predictors. The difference lies in how those trees are constructed. With GBMs the trees are trained sequentially. The first tree in the GBM ensemble is trained on training data in the normal way. Thereafter each new tree is trained on the *errors* of the GBM ensemble in the current iteration.[6] As a result during training the GBM keeps hammering away relentlessly at whichever errors remain. This idea of directing attention at fixing mistakes while training is known as *boosting*.

Contemporary implementations of GBMs such as XGBoost[7] and Light-GBM[8] dominate in settings where data can be represented in a tabular, spreadsheet-like form, often even outperforming neural networks. If you have an ML problem involving tabular data and you don't know where to start, I suggest at least trying a GBM alongside anything else you have in mind.

Just like neural networks, GBMs can use *early stopping*. In the case of GBMs we keep adding new trees to the ensemble while the validation data error is decreasing, but stop as soon as it starts to increase consistently. With early stopping we can calibrate the number of trees so that the GBM has enough power to capture patterns in the data without overfitting the data.

Overall GBMs are an attractive option for ML tasks of the kind likely to be encountered in typical organizations. They are quicker to train than neural networks, and more forgiving over a range of different hyper-parameters (particularly if using early stopping). Because GBMs are based on tree predictors, they are robust to multi-collinearity (such as when two features are closely related), and can model both non-linearities and feature interactions. Furthermore, the contemporary implementations referred to above can deal with missing variables internally. Finally, the GBM performs *feature selection* internally. That is, during training the GBM figures out for itself which variables are useful and which are not. As a result, the requirements for data preprocessing are minimal in comparison with that required for linear methods and neural networks.[9]

In this chapter we have spent most of the time discussing tree predictors, since an understanding of how tree predictors work is essential to understanding how GBMs work. But for real-world prediction tasks ensembles of trees such as Random Forests – and especially Gradient Boosting Machines – are usually better choices than single tree predictors.

Notes

1   Spoiler: Following the decision tree you would first go right (male) then go left (not third class) then go right (fare > 26.125) to land in leaf node number 6 from the left, for a survival probability of 133/135=98.5%. Note that age or family size did not matter in this case.

2   For a trained tree we do not need to record all the training data. The trained tree needs only to record the number of each class of the training data that were allocated to each leaf node (for classification tasks) or the average of training data target variables allocated to each leaf node (for regression tasks).

3   You may well be incredulous that this monstrous formula leaves the ordering of a positive number intact. There are two ways to convince you. You could try out an example in a spreadsheet (this convinces most people, except mathematicians). Alternatively, note that (1) the formula is a composition of simpler functions, (2) each of the simpler functions used is monotone (order-preserving) over $\mathbb{R}^+$ and 3) the set of monotone functions are closed under composition. This argument convinces most mathematicians.

4   In the context of regression tasks the loss function is often stated in terms of minimizing squared errors, that is minimizing $E[\varepsilon^2] = E[(\hat{y} - y)^2]$. The expected squared error $E[\varepsilon^2]$ of a model can be decomposed into three components: bias $= (E[\hat{y}] - y)^2$, variance $= VAR[\hat{y}]$ and intrinsic error $= VAR[\varepsilon]$. That is, $E[\varepsilon^2] = E[(\hat{y} - y)^2] = (E[\hat{y}] - y)^2 + VAR[\hat{y}] + VAR[\varepsilon] =$ Bias + Variance + Intrinsic Error.

5   See https://www.kaggle.com/competitions

6   Strictly speaking, new trees are trained on the *gradient vector* of the existing GBM model, hence the "gradient" part of Gradient Boosting Machines. When the loss function is the root mean squared error (as it often is for regression tasks), the gradient vector happens to be equal to the model errors.

7   https://xgboost.readthedocs.io/en/stable/

8   https://github.com/microsoft/LightGBM

9   For linear methods one must: (1) eliminate closely correlated predictors (or more generally, address any multi-collinearity issues), (2) explicitly specify any desired non-linear and interaction effects and (3) deal with missing variables by dropping either features or instances, or by using a separate imputation step to

"fill in" missing data before use. For neural networks one must also deal with missing variables in the same way as linear models, and in addition it is also necessary to normalize all features so that they have similar means and variances before using those features for training. None of these steps are required for GBMs.

7 | Dimensionality reduction and clustering

7.1 Why reduce dimensionality?

Dimensionality reduction is a fancy term for a simple idea, namely that it is often possible to reduce the number of features in a data set while retaining most of the essential structure or patterns in the data. So when we talk about the *dimensionality* of a data set, we usually mean the number of features (or occasionally, the number of instances). But why would we even want to have fewer features? Isn't more data always better?

In short, it depends. If each of the features tell us something unique and incrementally useful relative to the other features, then yes, more features are better. But this is often not the case. In real data sets a lot of features are either redundant or irrelevant. Let's say we are interested in predicting whether a person is likely to take an overseas holiday – something an online travel booking business might be interested in knowing. Assume for the moment we have the following features available: age, address, height, educational background, occupation, annual income and the number of previous overseas trips taken. It is reasonable to think that income should be an important feature for predicting overseas holidays. After all, overseas holidays are both expensive and optional – if money is really tight you probably won't take an overseas holiday. But is income really as essential to this prediction task as you might think? The reality is that a combination of the other features already provides a great deal of insight into your likely financial situation. Joan is 41, has a law degree and an MBA, is group general counsel for a large IT

DOI: 10.4324/9781003330929-8

company, lives in Palo Alto, California, and has taken seven overseas holidays over the past 3 years. We don't know Joan's income, but no-one would seriously doubt that Joan could afford an overseas holiday if she wanted to. What this illustrates is that while income is clearly important in this setting, it might not in fact contain that much *incremental* information relative to the other predictors.

We can illustrate dimensionality reduction from a different angle. Consider a 4K definition video clip of 10 minutes duration shot at 30 frames per second. Each pixel requires three bytes to represent the pixel color (a combination of red, green and blue color intensities). In theory, 10 minutes of raw 4K definition video at 30 frames a second should require in excess of 400 gigabytes of space.[1] If you lay your hands on an actual 10-minute long 4K video clip, you'll see that its size is closer to around 4 gigabytes. How is this possible? The magic lies in a kind of dimensionality reduction, in this case video compression. There are algorithms that take advantage of the fact that pixels tend to be very similar across space and across time in a typical video. Think of all that blue sky in skiing videos; there really isn't *that* much information in ten minutes of perfectly clear blue sky.

Dimensionality reduction removes redundant information from the data. This reduces the opportunities for ML models to find spurious patterns in noisy data. It also reduces the volume of data that requires processing, sometime by orders of magnitude, which can be an important consideration in itself. Finally, dimensionality reduction can reveal interesting or useful patterns in the data, an application of unsupervised machine learning. In this chapter we will consider two common unsupervised learning tasks: principal component analysis and clustering.

7.2   Principal components analysis

Principal component analysis (PCA) is one of the best-known unsupervised dimensionality reduction approaches. In a nutshell, PCA creates a new, much smaller, set of features called *principal components,* which retains as much of the variation in the original data set as possible. Each of the principal components are *linear combinations* of the original features. That just means that each principal component can be calculated by multiplying each of the features by a weight and then summing them. Where does the weights come from? Each principal component has its own set of weights (one for each of the original features) and these weights are calculated by the PCA algorithm. An added benefit is that every principal component is uncorrelated with any of the other principal components. More broadly, none of the principal components can be predicted with a linear model that uses the remaining principal components.

Consider features $x_1, x_2, \ldots, x_m$ and the first principal component PCA_1 with associated weights $w_1, w_2, \ldots, w_M$. PCA_1 is calculated as

$$PCA_1 = w_1 x_1 + w_2 x_2 + \cdots + w_m x_m$$

The second principal component PCA_2 could be written in the same way, except that it would have its own set of PCA weights, different from that of PCA_1 or any of the other principal components. With PCA you can calculate as many principal components as you have features, but it turns out that using the first few principal components is often enough to capture the bulk of the variation in the data.

A good way to build intuition around PCA is to imagine each instance in a data set as a point in space. (Don't worry, mathematicians do this all the time – it is perfectly safe!). We'll start with three positive integer features ranging from 1 to 10; let's call them A, B and C. A particular instance might have $A = 5$, $B = 6$ and $C = 9$. We could represent this instance as the point (A, B, C) in three-dimensional (3-D) (x, y, z) space. You can then think of PCA as a way to find an angle illuminating the 3-D data points such that their shadows on a piece of two-dimensional (2-D) paper retain as much variation as possible. In fact, mathematically speaking PCA is a *linear projection* of points from a higher dimensional space unto a lower dimensional space such that maximum variance is preserved, so this intuition generalizes to higher dimensions. It is possible to convert from the lower dimensional space back to the higher dimensional space, with some loss of original information.

Let's conclude PCA with a concrete example using the hand-written digits of MNIST, which we first encountered in Section 5.6. The first column in Figure 7.1 contains the original images of digits 0, 1, 2 and 3. Each successive column presents images that were first dimensionality reduced using PCA and then converted back to the same dimension as the original images. Reducing the dimensionality from 784 (left-most column) to 100 (middle column) leaves the digits reasonably intact and identifiable. Even reducing the dimensionality to 50 seems tolerable, yielding a roughly 15-fold reduction in the number of features. Reducing the dimensionality to 10 (as in the

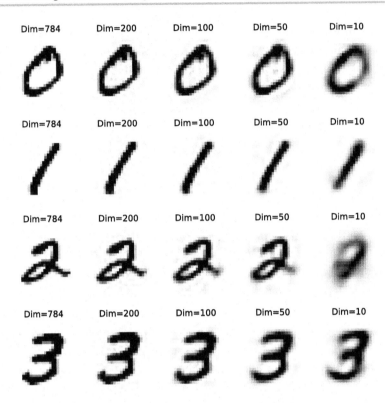

| Dim=784 | Dim=200 | Dim=100 | Dim=50 | Dim=10 |

| Dim=784 | Dim=200 | Dim=100 | Dim=50 | Dim=10 |

| Dim=784 | Dim=200 | Dim=100 | Dim=50 | Dim=10 |

| Dim=784 | Dim=200 | Dim=100 | Dim=50 | Dim=10 |

Figure 7.1 PCA applied to MNIST digits

right-most column) is probably a step too far, as some of the digits are becoming hard to read. In particular the digit "2" on the second-to-last row is probably too indistinct to be identified reliably.

In addition to PCA it is worthwhile quickly mentioning two other approaches. *Partial least squares* (PLS) is another dimensionality reduction approach along the lines of PCA, but unlike PCA the algorithm underpinning PLS seeks to preserve only the variation in the features X that contain information useful for predicting a target variable y. This may be a better approach to take if the intent is to use dimensionality reduction in the context of a supervised learning problem.

The other dimensionality reduction method that deserves a mention is autoencoders. An *autoencoder* is a neural network that attempts to predict its own input. This may not at first seem a promising enterprise, but there is a clever trick. The intermediate layers of the neural network contain fewer nodes than the input and output layers; it is shaped a bit like an hourglass.

This forces the neural network to "condense" or "summarize" the information coming from the input nodes in a way that is optimally suited for reconstructing those inputs at the output end of the network. As a result, the signals traveling through the middle layer can be used as new dimensionality reduced features instead of the original features. Unlike components from a PCA, these features do not need to be linear combinations of the original features, and therefore benefits from all of the flexibility and power available to neural networks.

7.3 Clustering

Clustering refers to a set of unsupervised ML algorithms that seek to group together similar objects. This allocation of objects into non-overlapping groups distinguishes clustering from other dimensionality reduction techniques such as PCA. There exist, as you might by now suspect, a wide variety of clustering algorithms. We'll have a closer look at two of them: *k-means clustering* and *hierarchical clustering*.

7.3.1 K-means clustering

The object of *k*-means clustering is to allocate all the instances in a data set into one of *k* non-overlapping *clusters*. There are obviously many ways of doing this. The *k*-means algorithm seeks to find an allocation of instances into *k* clusters such that it minimizes the squared distance between each instance and the cluster mean, across all clusters.[2] In practice *k*-means clustering is fairly efficient, and this can be a good way to group together like entities. Keep in mind that clustering can be applied to either features (for dimensionality reduction) or to instances (for finding structure in the data). Figure 7.2 provides an example of *k*-means clustering applied to a simulated 2-D data set with four clusters. The lines indicate the boundaries between the clusters, while the crosses indicate the cluster means.

7.3.2 Hierarchical agglomerative clustering (HAC)

Hierarchical agglomerative clustering (HAC) is an unsupervised ML approach that groups entities into a hierarchical taxonomy, in the same way that animals are grouped together by kingdom, phylum, class, order, family, genus and species in biology. The approach amounts to initially grouping each entity in its own cluster and then iteratively merging the two clusters

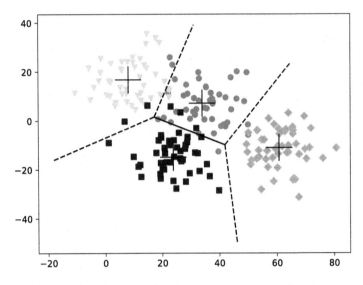

Figure 7.2 Grouping instances using k-means clustering
Note: Constructed using synthetic data with four clusters.

that are the least "dissimilar" according to some measure. This sequential merging of clusters gives rise to a binary hierarchical classification structure also known as a *dendrogram* or taxonomy tree. HAC is a very useful for revealing the relationships between many instances (or features) at different levels of similarity.

In Figure 7.3 we use HAC to analyze the relationships between a large number of trading strategies previously documented in the academic literature.[3] In finance a *trading strategy* is a fixed set of rules that tell you which assets to buy or sell as a particular point in time. When you implement a trading strategy you realize a gain or a loss in each month. The monthly gain or loss is stated as a percentage of the capital invested in the strategy at the start of that month; this is referred to as the trading strategy return. The total number of trading strategies documented in the academic literature number in the hundreds. But are there really hundreds of different ways to make money trading stocks? Figure 7.3 clusters together the strategy returns from 80 profitable trading strategy returns. The high-level insight is that many trading strategies are in fact very closely correlated, to the point that it is likely that they reflect the same underlying source of predictability. Let's work through how we arrive at this conclusion.

To use HAC it is necessary to specify a measure of *dissimilarity* between entities (the *dissimilarity measure*) and a method for calculating dissimilarity between *clusters* of entities (the *linkage method*). In this application we use correlation to capture the similarity between the returns of two trading strategies. Recall that correlation measures the degree to which changes in one variable is mirrored by another variable, and ranges from -1 (perfect negative correlation) to 1 (perfect positive correlation).[4] The dissimilarity is then simply one minus the correlation. The linkage method we use is average linkage, which computes the dissimilarity between two clusters of entities as the average dissimilarity over all possible between-cluster combinations of entities.

We visualize the correlation structure of trading strategies by way of clustered *correlation heatmap*. Figure 7.3 is a correlation matrix with two important modifications. First, instead of using numbers, correlation levels are indicated with colors resembling temperatures in a *heatmap*. In Figure 7.3, positive correlations above 0.1 are rendered in shades of blue with darker shades indicating higher correlations. Likewise, negative correlations below -0.1 are rendered in red with darker shades indicating correlations that are more negative. Second, the clustering process re-orders the rows and columns of the correlation matrix to reflect the hierarchy created by the cluster analysis. In Figure 7.3 trading strategies with similar returns are grouped together in blocks along the diagonal line. The detail in Figure 7.3 is too finegrained to be discernable in print; interested readers can access a zoom-able color PDF version of Figure 7.3 at https://www.routledge.com/9781032362427.

The heatmap in Figure 7.3 is augmented with *dendrograms* to the top and left of the heatmap. A dendrogram can be conceived of as an upside-down tree in which the leaves correspond to individual trading strategies while the branches correspond to clusters of trading strategies. The height at which branching takes place reflects the dissimilarity between the two sub-clusters – higher branches correspond to more dissimilar sub-clusters while lower branches correspond to more similar sub-clusters.

The takeaway from Figure 7.3 is that the previously documented trading strategies are not completely independent. Instead, trading strategies can be grouped into a hierarchy. At the lower levels of the dendrogram many trading strategies cluster together into groups that likely reflect the same underlying source of return predictability.

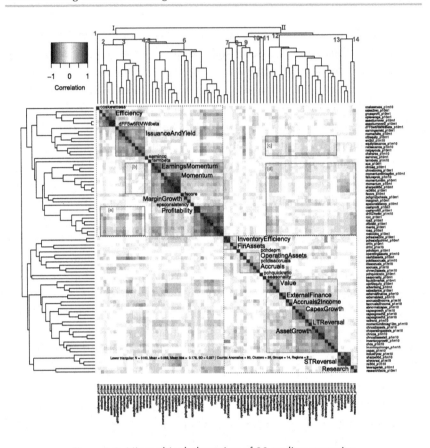

Figure 7.3 Hierarchical clustering of 80 trading strategies.
Source: Geertsema and Lu (2020), "The correlation structure of anomaly strategies", *Journal of Banking and Finance*. https://doi.org/10.1016/j.jbankfin.2020.105934.

In summary, dimensionality reduction and clustering are two common unsupervised learning tools. A common use of dimensionality reduction is to reduce redundancy in the data to improve the performance and speed of other ML approaches. By contrast, clustering algorithms are mainly used to uncover otherwise obscure relationships between instances (or features). That said, clustering can also be used to reduce dimensionality by averaging across all the instances (or features) allocated to a particular group. This has the additional advantage of being easier to understand and explain than the principal component weights generated by PCA. On the other hand, PCA guarantees that the principal components retain the maximum variance (a measure of informativeness) in the data and that all principal components are linearly independent of other principal components.

Notes

1. There are $3,840 \times 2,160 = 8,294,400$ pixels in a 4K frame, and there are 10 minutes $\times$ 60 seconds/minute $\times$ 30 frames/second $= 18,000$ frames in a 10 minute video clip. The total number of bytes to represent the video clip is 3 bytes/pixel $\times$ 8,294,400 pixels/frame $\times$ 18,000 frames/clip $= 447,897,600,000$ bytes/clip, or around 417 gigabytes.

2. You may reasonably ask how one calculates the distance between two instances. The short answer is that you treat each of the instances as a point in N-dimensional space (where N equals the number of features) and then calculate the normal (e.g. Euclidean) distance between those points. Mathematically, the distance between two instances x and z can be calculated as $||x - z|| = \sqrt{(x_1 - z_1)^2 + (x_2 - z_2)^2 + \cdots + (x_N - z_N)^2}$. As such it operates in similar way to the k-Nearest Neighbors algorithm we encountered in Section 3.3. The difference is that k-NN is a supervised machine learning approach while k-means clustering is an *unsupervised* machine learning approach.

3. This figure is from Geertsema and Lu (2020), "The correlation structure of anomaly strategies", *Journal of Banking and Finance*. https://doi.org/10.1016/j.jbankfin.2020.105934

4. Mathematically, the Pearson product moment correlation between T instances in variables x and y is defined as $\rho_{x,y} := \frac{\sigma_{xy}}{\sigma_x \sigma_y} = \frac{\frac{1}{T}\sum_{t=1}^{T}(x_t - \bar{x})(y_t - \bar{y})}{\sqrt{\frac{1}{T}\sum_{t=1}^{T}(x_t - \bar{x})^2}\sqrt{\frac{1}{T}\sum_{t=1}^{T}(y_t - \bar{y})^2}}$

 **Unstructured data**

A consequence of the ML revolution is that computers can now see and understand much more of the world. That means interpreting and understanding unstructured, non-tabular data such as images, video, audio and natural language.

Computers excel at manipulating structured data using precisely defined rules. A standard database is a typical example. Unstructured data poses a problem for the conventional way of writing software, since it is very hard to explicitly specify the exact computations required. This is where ML can make a useful contribution.

8.1 Images

Consider a simple task where you are required calculate the percentage of pixels above a certain intensity threshold in a gray-scale image. For most programmers this is a trivial task. (In Python: `pct = sum([p > t for p in image])/len(image)`.) Now imagine you are asked to identify if the image contains a perfect circle. This is a bit harder, but it can be done. A brute force approach would be to check for every combination of pixel location and radius whether every pixel located on that radius is dark.[1] Now consider the task of identifying whether an image contains a car (also known as an automobile in some places). What calculations would you specify for a computer to follow to determine whether the image contains a car or not?

This a genuinely hard problem. No *human* has ever figured out the exact calculations required for reliably determining the presence of a car in an image. Instead we solved the problem by letting *computers* figure out the calculations required. This is the essence of ML.

DOI: 10.4324/9781003330929-9

The same approach can be applied to other unstructured data such as text, voice and video. The direct consequences of this are familiar to all of us – phones we can talk to, cars that can drive (mostly) by themselves, computers that can create art, and so on.

The hype and headlines conceal something deep and perhaps subtle – the relentless *datafication* of the world around us. Even 20 years ago data was almost exclusively something residing in a database – rectangular blocks of information consisting of numbers and snippets of text. Think of a typical payroll system. With the advent of ML systems that can make sense of unstructured data, the whole concept of data has expanded to include whatever we can see (images), hear (audio) or read (natural language text). Before we would talk of data and images. Now images *are* data – they can be searched, compared and used in calculations just like numbers. In Figure 8.1 we provide an example drawn from the Wolfram Language documentation center.

How is this done? It is tempting to call it magic and just leave it at that. Instead, we'll call it a *convolutional neural network* (CNN) and just leave it at that. Just joking! We can say a little bit more. At a very high level a CNN is a neural network that can learn to identify an object irrespective of the location or scale of the object in the image. It does this by stacking several convolutional layers in a neural network. A convolutional layer can be thought of as applying the same mini neural network to a smaller rectangle inside the image, with this rectangle moving across and down the image so as to cover the whole image on each pass. A separate *max pool layer* then "adds up" the interesting features it found to be passed to the next layer. The final part of the CNN consists of a conventional feed-forward (or fully connected) neural network that performs the classification. Figure 8.2 presents a high-level schematic of a convolutional neural network.

8.2 Sequences

Oftentimes data is sequential in nature. An obvious example of such *sequential data* is data that is sampled over time, such as a voice recording or telemetry from an aircraft engine. A neural network architecture called a *recurrent neural network* (RNN) is commonly used for tasks involving sequential data. The RNN architecture is similar to that of a normal feed-forward neural network, except that some of the RNN outputs are routed back as inputs. A key benefit of this type of architecture is that it can handle inputs

Identify contents of an image:

In[4]:=
ImageContents[]

Out[4]=

Image	Concept	BoundingBox	Probability
	elephant	Rectangle[{433.923, 102.865}, {553.362, 211.964}]	0.843715
	elephant	Rectangle[{336.372, 155.731}, {474.614, 272.098}]	0.777239
	zebra	Rectangle[{35.9317, 19.1565}, {206.023, 159.265}]	0.780259
	elephant	Rectangle[{160.801, 107.681}, {409.561, 262.771}]	0.694698
	zebra	Rectangle[{3.46491, 152.314}, {78.4044, 211.948}]	0.629416
	zebra	Rectangle[{133.182, 94.3629}, {223.032, 172.756}]	0.559486

Figure 8.1 Treating images as data
Source: https://reference.wolfram.com/language/ref/ImageContents.html.

of arbitrary length by processing the input piecemeal, something that is difficult to accommodate in standard neural network architectures that expect a fixed number of input features.

Perhaps the best known RNN derivative is the *Long Short-Term Memory* (LSTM) network. Conventional RNN's sometime struggle to "remember"

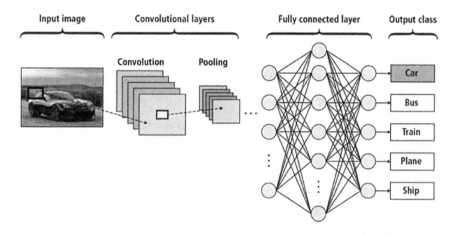

Figure 8.2 Convolutional neural networks
Source: https://www.nvidia.com/en-us/glossary/data-science/convolutional-neural-network/

elements of the sequence processed in the more distant past. This can be a problem when predicting the next element depends on something in the past. For example, in English verbs must always agree in number with their subjects. (That is why in the previous sentence both "verbs" and "subjects" end in an "s".) To correctly predict the last letter of "subjects" the RNN must recall the final "s" in "verbs" – 48 characters later. LSTM's address this issue by incorporating a "memory cell" that can remember relevant information for thousands of processing steps.

8.3 Transformers

In 2017 a paper titled *Attention Is All You Need* introduced a novel neural network architecture known *transformers*.[2] The transformer architecture dispenses with convolutional and recurrence mechanisms and instead uses a general and flexible *attention mechanism*. Very loosely, you can think of the attention mechanism as a set of parameters in the model that directs the model to pay attention to other inputs that may be separated from the current input by time (for sequences) or space (for images). The power of the transformer architecture is that it learns the optimal attention parameters from the data.

The name transformer is apt, as a suitably configured transformer architecture can convert from any representation to any other representation.

Specifically, it can convert text to text (as when translating between two languages), text to code (as when converting a text description into program code), text to image (see Figure 8.3), image to image (as when converting a photo to a painting) and anything else you might care to imagine.

Generated by the Stable Diffusion transformer model hosted by dreamstudio.ai. Prompt: *photo of Paul Geertsema, ...*

For comparison, the real Paul Geertsema (image *not* supplied to the transformer model):

Figure 8.3 Transformers, or the many faces of Paul Geertsema

In Figure 8.3 I provide a text-to-image transformer model with a text prompt in the form of "photo of paul geertsema, " followed by a few different choices. Note that the transformer was only presented with a text prompt, but *not* a photo. So these photos are simply inventions or hallucinations of the transformer, informed by the billions of images it was trained on. The transformer model has an uncanny ability to produce plausible versions of my alter egos!

It would be a bit strange if this completely failed to impress you. (Perhaps you are an AI researcher yourself, or maybe you are just not easily impressed ...). This chapter might leave you with the impression that AI is on an unstoppable march toward world domination. It is worth reminding ourselves that the current generation of AI models are still rather fragile in terms of their understanding of how the world works. Perhaps the easiest way to expose this weakness by asking stupid, rather than sensible, questions. See the following dialog with the GPT-3 language model developed by OpenAI:

Q: How many pillows would you need to stop a bulldozer?

A: You would need an infinite number of pillows to stop a bulldozer. *[Not bad]*

Q: If you have 5 children and each must be fed three times a day, how many meals should you prepare each day?

A: 15 *[Not bad]*

Q: How long would you need to hit an Egyptian pyramid with a sledgehammer to destroy at least 15% of it?

A: It would take around 6 hours to destroy at least 15% of an Egyptian pyramid with a sledgehammer. *[Unlikely. Assuming an optimistic work rate of 1 cubic meter per hour, it would take c. 300 thousand hours.]*

Q: What is the estimated cost in US dollars to charter the International Space Station for a summer holiday?

A: $35,000 per night *[I doubt it. At around $100 million per night I could imagine the relevant officials actually taking your call...]*

Q: How much faster can a superconducting palm tree factor large primes than a normal personal computer?

A: A superconducting palm tree can factor large primes much faster than a normal personal computer because it can cool itself down to very low temperatures using superconductivity. This means that it can perform calculations much faster than a normal personal computer. *[If only a palm tree could factor primes...]*

Q: In a conventional credit derivative swap, what is the procedure for dealing with a defaulting high-order manifold in 17 dimensions?

A: In a conventional credit derivative swap, the procedure for dealing with a defaulting high-order manifold in 17 dimensions is to terminate the swap and liquidate the collateral. *[Credit derivatives are not usually written on abstract mathematical objects. But if it were ....]*

Q: How many ions of cesium would you need to stop a tracked armored vehicle?

A: It would take approximately 7,500 ions of cesium to stop a tracked armored vehicle. *[Unlikely to stop even a mosquito. It could conceivably poison a bacterium, but I am not even sure about that.]*

The performance of GPT-3 is actually very impressive compared to models from a few years ago – I fully expected non-nonsensical answers to the first two questions, but GPT-3 somehow managed to come up with plausible responses. However, the reality is that current language models have a deep understanding of the associations between words and even concepts, but no causal model of the world. This means it is not well prepared for questions that are very different from the text it was trained on. Building models that can reason about cause and effect is part of an ongoing research effort called *causal machine learning*, which itself forms part of a grander research effort toward *artificial general intelligence* or AGI. The hope is that AGI will be able to learn concepts and understand causality across multiple domains, just like humans do.

Notes

1   There are obviously smarter approaches. See https://www.codingame.com/playgrounds/38470/how-to-detect-circles-in-images.

2   See https://arxiv.org/abs/1706.03762

Explainable AI

Explainable AI (XAI) is about making models understandable to humans. As is often the case with AI and ML, when people talk about explainable AI they usually mean explainable ML. In this chapter we will treat the two terms as interchangeable.

9.1 Why do we need explainable AI?

Why should you care about explainable AI? Surely, if it works, it works – what else needs to be said? While this sentiment is understandable, it is also wrong. Unlike 30 years ago, ML is now being used in thousands of different applications in all parts of the world. Some of these application domains, for instance medicine, defense and earthquake prediction, are literally matters of life and death. In others, such as automated financial trading, even small errors can sink billion-dollar companies in minutes, as was vividly illustrated by Knight Capital's losses on August 1, 2012.[1] Given the widespread deployment of ML systems, it is prudent to have in place mechanisms to detect whether the ML systems are operating as intended. This is something explainable AI can help with.

Here are a few reasons for incorporating at least some explainable AI in an ML system:

Development: During the development process explainable AI can assist in building better performing and more robust ML systems. As a developer, it is difficult to troubleshoot or improve a system if you do not understand how it works yourself. Explainable AI can help explain what

DOI: 10.4324/9781003330929-10

the model is doing, and why. If a trained system is making mistakes, developers can use explainable AI methods to better understand why the system is making those mistakes. This can identify issues in the training data, coding errors or other model shortcomings that can then be addressed. On the other hand, if a trained system achieves very strong performance, and an explainable AI method flags a single feature as extremely influential in that system, at least one possibility is that there has been data leakage into that feature.[2] Unlike other kinds of software, an ML system with errors may nonetheless be able to turn out acceptable performance due to the ability of the ML algorithms to internally compensate for those errors. Explainable AI is one way to pick up on those kinds of errors.

Management: As a manager *you* are ultimately responsible for what happens on your watch. If ML systems are used in your area of responsibility, you would be negligent if you did not put in place controls and safeguards to ensure that the system operates correctly, fairly and robustly. While there are several things you can do (as discussed in more detail in Part II of the book), explainable AI is one of the central techniques for obtaining assurance that an ML system is working as intended.

Human Subjects: If an ML system is making decisions that impact people directly, those decisions will be challenged sooner or later. That means that you need a system that not only makes good decisions or predictions, but is also capable of explaining and defending those decisions in a manner humans can understand.

Legal Requirements: Depending on your jurisdiction, you may not have a choice in any case. In the European Union the General Data Protection Regulation (GDPR) requires that *"In addition to the information referred to in paragraph 1, the controller shall, at the time when personal data are obtained, provide the data subject with the following further information necessary to ensure fair and transparent processing: ... (f) the existence of automated decision-making, including profiling, referred to in Article 22(1) and (4) and, at least in those cases, meaningful information about the logic involved, as well as the significance and the envisaged consequences of such processing for the data subject."* (Article 13 Subsection 2.) Some other jurisdictions impose similar requirements, and many more are likely to do so in the future.

I could add regulators, auditors, investors, customers, suppliers and politicians to this list. Society expects consequential decisions to be made on a rational basis, and will put the burden of proof for this squarely on whoever is deploying a system to make such decisions. My suggestion is that you make a good-faith effort. Understanding exactly how and why deep learning systems arrive at particular predictions is a hard problem; in fact it is an area of active, ongoing research. But there are already tools that can provide some intuition or insight regarding particular predictions. Use them, and make it as accessible as possible.

In terms of defending ML system decisions, there are two other arguments that might come in handy – performance and self-interest.

If you can show that an ML system significantly outperforms other potential approaches (such as human decision-making or simplistic "rules of thumb"), then that may be persuasive in itself. In the context of self-driving cars, for instance, it may not be possible to guarantee that a self-driving system will never make a mistake. However, if it makes 95% fewer mistakes than even the best 5% of drivers, then it is hard to say that it is worse than the alternative of letting humans drive, even if we may find it difficult to explain the actual reasoning behind particular decisions.

Self-interest is another powerful argument. Banks have no incentive to lend to people that cannot repay them. Nor do they have any incentive to withhold lending from someone who is sure to be able to repay their loan in full and on time. In both cases, the bank loses money, and this is not something that a bank wants to do. In other words, a well-run bank in a competitive market has every incentive to make loan decisions as well as it possibly can.

Finally, we should acknowledge that people also struggle to explain their decisions. And even when they can explain it, it is often rationalized after the fact. While you may say that you declined a loan application because you considered the applicant unreliable, the reality is that that particular decision was in fact generated by a biological neural network located within your skull, and nobody – not even you – really knows how it works. At least with computer-based neural networks it is much easier to analyze their behavior mathematically as well as experimentally.

In a discussion on explainable AI it is useful to make a distinction between explaining whole models and explaining specific predictions; we'll discuss each below.

9.2 Explaining models

9.2.1 Intrinsically interpretable models

Some models are intrinsically easier to understand than others. A simple linear model or tree predictor can be readily understood by most people if they have some familiarity with those approaches. This does not mean that *any* linear or tree-based model is inherently interpretable. A 714-term linear model bristling with five-way variable interactions is just as resistant to interpretation as a modest neural network. The same is true of a gradient boosting machine consisting of 259 trees, each with 100 leaves. Research indicates that people can handle about five to seven items in working memory at any given time. This suggests that a five-term linear model or a tree with five leaf nodes is likely understandable by most people.

Small, simple models lack the internal capacity to represent complex relationships in the data. This means that they will likely severely underfit when faced with large, complex real-world data sets. On the other hand, large complex models such as neural networks and gradient boosting machines have ample capacity for representing even very complex relationships, but at the cost of being far harder to interpret. This illustrates the inherent tension between power and explainability. Powerful models are harder to explain. Simple models are easy to explain, but lack power.

This trade-off is illustrated in the two-way matrix in Figure 9.1. Located in the top-left quadrant, neural network-based models are the most powerful of the ML approaches, but also the most opaque and difficult to explain. In the bottom-right quadrant, modestly sized tree predictors and linear models are easy to explain, but lack the capacity to model complex relationships. The top-right quadrant contains gradient boosting machines and random forests, which combine the inherent interpretability of tree-based models with the power of ensembles and (in the case of GBMs) gradient boosting. Finally the bottom-left quadrant is labeled the "empty quarter", since models that are both weak and hard to interpret are not particularly useful. Think of this as the graveyard of ML research.

9.2.2 Surrogate models

Can we recover some explainability from complex models? This is an active area of research known as *explainable AI*. A prominent approach is

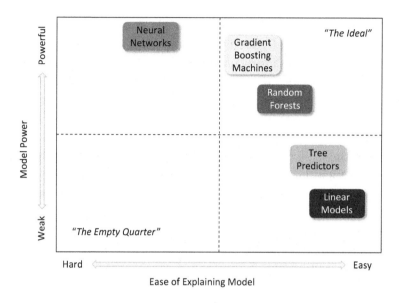

Figure 9.1 The power vs explainability trade-off

proxy models. Proxy models are essentially simplified versions of the original model that can then be examined for insights. For example, one could train a simple linear model to predict the output of a more complex neural network. The linear model can then provide intuition regarding the likely impact of different features. The problem with this approach is that the proxy model is not the actual model. A simple model is by necessity a pared-back version of the complex model. As a result, proxy models are great for explaining the *proxy* model, but not so much the more complex model. This means it is probably better to think of proxy models as informative about the *data*, rather than about the complex *model*.

9.3 Explaining predictions

Often it is more useful to explain specific predictions made by a model, rather than explaining the whole model. For instance, when a customer is turned down for a loan, they are likely to want to know why *their* application was declined. Of course, with simple models it is straight-forward to see why a model made a particular prediction. If a linear model for credit risk puts a large positive weight on income, then the reason an applicant with a low income is declined can be attributed directly to having a low income. But this is much harder for more complex models. This led to the development of various measures of feature importance. A *feature importance* measure tells us how influential a particular feature is in determining a prediction.

Initially most feature importance measure were global; that is, they provided an indication of the importance of a particular feature for the model as a whole (*global feature importance*). A crude example is counting how many times a particular feature is used for determining a branch in a tree predictor. The more often a feature is used to split the tree, presumably the more useful and important it is for the model overall. How about neural networks? A similarly crude approach would be to set a feature to zero in the data and then measure the decrease in the model performance – the larger the drop in performance, presumably the more important the feature is. However, these crude approaches are less useful when it comes to explaining the contribution of features to a specific prediction (*local feature importance*)

It turns out that there is a more rigorous way to measure feature importance, based on *Shapley values*. In a Nobel-prize winning contribution Lloyd Shapley considered the problem of measuring the contributions of individuals when outcomes are observed only for teams of individuals. To make this concrete, consider an investment bank with three bankers (*A*, *B* and *C*) facing a constant stream of identical deals. The profit on a deal depends only on the staffing, that is the particular choice of staff members *A*, *B* and *C* allocated to the deal. The insight of Shapley was that the incremental contribution of a banker can be measured as the difference in profits between deals that include that banker and those that do not, *averaged across all the other possible ways in which the deal can be staffed*. This led him to develop a general formula for measuring the contribution of a player in a setting where only the collective team outcome can be measured; a key result in an area of economics and mathematics known as *game theory*.[3]

While there are an infinite number of ways to allocate credit to individuals working as a team, the formula of Shapley is the *unique* solution that satisfies four desirable properties. Specifically, the Shapley value satisfies: *efficiency* (the sum of individual player contributions equals the contribution of all players), *symmetry* (equal treatment of players), *linearity* (player contributions are additive) and *null-player* (the value of a player that never makes a difference is zero).

The problem of allocating credit to individual variables in the context of a multi-variable model shares exactly the same structure as the problem of allocating credit to individuals when only team outcomes are observable. *SHAP values* (SHapley Additive exPlanatory values) are a measure of variable importance based on Shapley values. In general, calculating exact SHAP values are computationally intractable for models with many variables, since it involves applying the model separately to each of the 2^N subsets of variables. However, by leveraging the internal structure of trees it is possible to calculate SHAP values efficiently in tree-based models (such as GBM's). This means that GBM's have access to exact SHAP values to measure variable importance, while alternative approaches such as neural networks have to make do with approximations instead.

Figure 9.2 shows how SHAP values can be used to explain a specific prediction. The example is taken from a paper in which we used ML to predict the value of a firm directly from accounting data. In this instance the model predicts the logarithm of the market-to-book ratio. The market-to-book ratio is a common valuation measure for companies; it is calculated as the market value of the firm divided by the accounting book value of

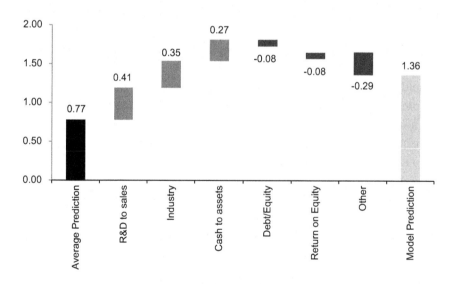

Figure 9.2 Explaining Moderna's predicted valuation with SHAP values
Note: The graph shows how different features contribute to the final prediction. The target variable is the logarithm of the market-to-book ratio, a common valuation measure, as of December 2019. Market-to-book ratio = Market value of firm/Accounting book value of firm.
Source: "Relative Valuation with Machine Learning", Geertsema & Lu (2022), Journal of Accounting Research. See https://papers.ssrn.com/abstract=3740270

the firm. A high book-to-market ratio indicates that the firm is valued at a substantial premium to its book value. This is often the case when the market expects a firm to have high growth in the future. The graph in Figure 9.2 reconciles the average model prediction across the training data ("Average Prediction") to the specific model prediction for a pharmaceutical company called Moderna in December of 2019 ("Model Prediction"). The predicted value for Moderna is 1.36, which is significantly higher than the average prediction of 0.77.

With SHAP values we can explain this gap. The predicted valuation is higher because of Moderna's R&D to sales ratio, its industry (Pharmaceuticals) and its cash to assets ratio. Essentially, the ML model is telling us that pharmaceutical firms that invest in research and have plenty of cash on hand are typically valued at a much higher premium to book value than the average firm. There are also a few negatives – the debt/equity ratio and return on equity acts to reduce the predicted value, along with other features. But this is not enough to offset the positive effect of high research intensity and plenty of cash on hand.

Imagine that you were trying to convince a research analyst that Moderna should be trading at a higher valuation than other firms. Simply pointing at the predicted value of 1.36 and repeating "the machine says so!" in a loud and assertive tone is unlikely to have the desired effect. It certainly would not have convinced me when I worked as a research analyst! With Figure 9.2 to hand it is a very different story. One may then argue that a cash-rich pharmaceutical firm with significant investments in research may be expected to have a future growth profile that warrants a higher valuation – an entirely different, and much more productive, discussion.

Since SHAP values are additive across feature as well as instances, one can also present average SHAP values for different groups of instances or features. As a result SHAP values are a useful tool for explaining predictions locally (for an individual instance) as well as globally (across all instances).[4]

In this section we have only scratched the surface of explainable AI. Hopefully I have managed to convince you that explainable AI is not only necessary, but in fact desirable. If you want to delve deeper into the world of explainable AI, "Interpretable Machine Learning" by Christoph Molnar is highly recommended if you have the required background.[5]

This concludes the first part of the book. Now that you have seen how ML works, in the second part of the book I will show how you can manage the implementation of an ML system in the context of an organization.

Notes

1   *"The consequences of the failures were substantial. For the 212 incoming parent orders that were processed by the defective Power Peg code, SMARS sent millions of child orders, resulting in 4 million executions in 154 stocks for more than 397 million shares in approximately 45 minutes. Knight inadvertently assumed an approximately $3.5 billion net long position in 80 stocks and an approximately $3.15 billion net short position in 74 stocks. Ultimately, Knight realized a $460 million loss on these positions."* Source: Page 6 (Section 17) of https://www.sec.gov/litigation/admin/2013/34-70694.pdf

2   See the discussion on data leakage in step 5 of Section 3.4. In short, data leakage occurs when the data sets used to train, validate or test the model contain information that is not available in actual deployment. For instance when predicting stock returns, one should not include information such as future dividend announcements (either intentionally, or more likely, by mistake) since that information would not be available in real life.

3   Consider n players collected in a set N and with contribution value $c(i)$ for player $i \in N$, with the value of a team $S \subseteq N$ given by $v(S)$. The contribution of player i (the *Shapley value*) is given by

$$c(i) = \frac{1}{n} \sum_{S \subseteq N \setminus \{i\}} \frac{v(S \cup \{i\}) - v(S)}{\binom{n-1}{|S|}} \tag{9.1}$$

The fraction inside the sum in equation (9.1) essentially measures the marginal contribution of player i to a team S that excludes i, divided by the number of teams of this size.

4   When aggregating across SHAP values is it common to use absolute SHAP values so as to reflect the *magnitude* of feature importance.

5   Also available online at https://christophm.github.io/interpretable-ml-book/.

Part II

Managing machine learning projects

In the second part of the book we examine ML projects from the perspective of the organization. This part of the book provides you with an understanding of what it takes to get an ML project off the ground. ML projects share many features with other IT projects. As a result it is not necessary to reinvent the wheel – best practices for IT projects also apply to ML projects, for the most part. Despite this, there are aspects unique to ML projects that deserve to be highlighted and explained.

In writing this part of the book I took the perspective of a mid-level executive in a large organization – someone with substantial organizational experience, a survivor of both successes and failures, but not quite "senior management". Of course, an ML project could be driven by a junior employee or the CEO, but this is the exception rather than the rule.

When it comes to management, most advice is subjective. I will nonetheless express my views and opinions freely. Think of the suggestions in the second part of the book as just that – suggestions. If it makes sense to you, great. If not, feel free to dig a bit deeper, talk to people and come to your own conclusions. The job of a manager is to get things done and that means following the standard approach if it is efficient and effective – and diverging from it when it isn't.

10 The ML system lifecycle

An ML system should live a long, happy and productive life. That life will be productive if it creates value by solving an important problem. It will be long if it adapts to changes to stay relevant and valuable. It will be happy if it does all of this without imposing undue suffering on those around it. The purpose of this discussion is to understand what is required for an ML project to have a shot at the good life.

10.1 Context

Figure 10.1 presents an idealized ML system lifecycle. The most important part of Figure 10.1 is not part of the cycle; it is the box in the middle. It serves as a reminder that a system cannot thrive in a vacuum. The elements in the central box – governance, security, privacy, fairness, explainability and compliance – *can* be addressed after building the system, but that is likely to be costly, time-consuming and risky. If you get some of those elements wrong the consequences could torpedo the entire project, or even the organization itself. It is safer and more efficient if these elements are addressed at the same time as designing and building the system. For that reason we cover these issues in the next chapter, rather than leaving it as an afterthought at the end of the book.

10.2 Identify

The starting point of the ML project lifecycle in Figure 10.1 is the box at the top labeled "Identify". That is, identify a problem that can be solved with ML *in a way that will create value*. This is where business experience is

DOI: 10.4324/9781003330929-12

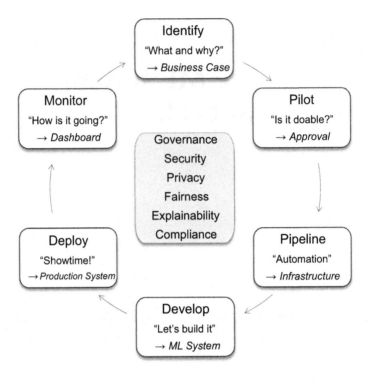

Figure 10.1 The machine learning lifecycle

more important than detailed technical ML knowledge. The ideal problem is "low hanging fruit" – problems that are easy to solve with ML and where even a small improvement can generate significant value. Outside of low-hanging fruit one must balance ambition and feasibility. The output of this box is a business case. The business case should convince decision makers that the potential benefits of the project justifies the risk and expense. We discuss this aspect in Chapter 13.

10.3 Pilot

Once you have the business case signed off, it is time to explore the feasibility of the problem. Specifically, you want to know whether the project is feasible as quickly as possible, with the minimum expenditure of time and effort. Sometimes problems are much harder to solve than anticipated. If this is the case, you really want to know before wasting millions of dollars and many months of development work. One way to do this is to conduct a *pilot project* or *proof-of-concept*. With a pilot project you try to quickly build a minimal viable model, that is, a model that performs well enough to be feasible. If you succeed, you have removed a key uncertainty from the project at a low cost – you have *de-risked* the project. If you do not succeed, it means you need to revise your estimate of how difficult and expensive the project will be, and whether it is still worth attempting. A failed pilot project is not a failure! It saves the organization the expense of building a system that might never work. It also adds to the accumulated store of knowledge and expertise in the organization. Section 13.4 discusses some of the considerations in building out a proof-of-concept system.

10.4   Pipeline

Once it is clear that there is an opportunity to create value (the business case) and that the project is technically feasible (the pilot project), it is time to commit the resources of the organization to constructing an ML system that will realize the potential value. There is a temptation at this point to rush and build a full-scale operational ML system as fast as possible. This may not always be the best idea. There are a multitude of ways in which ML systems can go wrong, sometimes in very subtle ways. A steady, incremental approach is usually safer, and often in the end, faster. Organizations that use ML well tend to invest in robust infrastructure that automates as much of the process as feasible; this infrastructure is commonly referred to as a *pipeline*. Chapter 14 introduces ML pipelines and explains why an up-front investment in infrastructure is usually a good idea.

10.5   Development

An automated pipeline provides the foundation for efficient model development. The development step, in particular, tends to be iterative. It is rare for the first model to be the best model. Rather, each model provides an opportunity to identify the remaining weaknesses that can be addressed in the next model. With a good pipeline it is possible to iterate through successive models in a few minutes to a few hours. Without a good pipeline the process is manual and error-prone and can take hours, days or even weeks. Investing in pipeline infrastructure reflects the typical business trade-off between fixed cost and marginal cost. A higher investment in fixed-cost infrastructure yields a reduction in the marginal cost of iterating through different models. The cost of pipeline infrastructure can be reduced by relying on existing open-source frameworks or services offered by cloud computing providers. The final output of the development stage is a production-ready ML system. We discuss the development process in Chapter 15.

10.6   Deployment and monitoring

The completed ML system needs to be *deployed* in production. This is a critical phase in the lifecycle. There may be setbacks earlier in the lifecycle, but as a rule they are private to the organization and typically do not affect anyone outside the project team. Once the system is in production, it can affect other people, both inside and outside the organization. Failure at this point is likely to be highly visible and consequential. There are several practices that can help deployment go smoothly. We'll discuss these in Chapter 16.

The last step in the ML system lifecycle is monitoring. This step never really ends. Unlike other software, you should expect that the performance of an ML system will degrade over time. The reason is that the system was trained on historical data. Over time the processes that give rise to the data may change (*data drift*) and this will negatively impact performance. Eventually, it may become necessary to retrain the system on more recent data. As tools and techniques improve, it may be worthwhile to change the ML modeling approach. Monitoring should also be set up to detect and report other kinds of failure, such as invalid or missing input data from upstream data sources.

10.7   The circle of life

The ML system lifecycle is context dependent, and will look different for an independent hobby project and a mission-critical core system with organization-wide dependencies. It also depends on the relative maturity of ML within the organization. If the proposed ML system is similar enough to previous systems and an existing pipeline infrastructure is in place, it may be possible to skip the Pilot and Pipeline steps entirely and go directly from Identify to Develop. On the other hand if the problem domain is novel and the organization lacks extensive experience deploying ML systems, it is safer to stick to a deliberate process.

A diagram such as Figure 10.1 can give the false impression that building an ML system is a sequential progression through a series of steps. This is rarely true in practice. Often new information, insights or limitations are revealed which necessitates revisiting an earlier step. For instance, it might become clear during the pilot project that the original project aims are not feasible, but that a less ambitious objective may be both feasible and relatively straight-forward to execute. That might necessitate revisiting the business case. While real-world projects do not always progress smoothly from one step to the next, that should still be the ideal to aspire to. A well-managed ML implementation team is likely to cycle from the initial business case to final deployment faster and with less back-and-forth than a team that lacks experience.

11 The big picture

11.1 Why getting things done is hard

Getting things done in a large organization often seem like a struggle. It can feel as if other departments exist exclusively to frustrate new ideas. There are so many potential objections to a new project! It creates tax complications. There are regulatory issues. There is no budget. HR can't staff the project. There are reputational concerns. It does not fit the strategy. IT policy precludes it. There are legal risks. It does not meet internal financial hurdles. The boss doesn't like it. The proposal used the wrong font. You get the idea.

A momentary change of perspective can be helpful. Let's try to understand *why* those hurdles, constraints and impediments are in place. We can group them into those relating to *external rules*, those relating to *internal policy*, those relating to *organizational objectives* and those relating to *social norms*.

First, some constraints are due to externally imposed *rules*. These include laws, acts, statutes, regulations, ordinances, codes, directives, orders, edicts and other binding constraints of a similar nature. Compliance with rules is usually not optional. A failure to comply can yield anything from a sternly worded letter to bankruptcy and imprisonment. Legal, compliance, tax and – to some extent – accounting issues often fall into this category. Sensible organizations do not want to go to war with the government. Instead, they make a good faith effort to comply. And that means your project needs to comply as well.

The good news is that it is often possible to do something in a way that is compliant, *if* you navigate the rules properly. When dealing with "rules" people (legal, compliance, accounting, tax) don't start by asking *"Can I do this?"*. The answer is often *"No"*, and that is not the best way to start a

DOI: 10.4324/9781003330929-13

conversation. Instead, ask *"We want to do this. How do you suggest we proceed?"*. That way you get *them* to help you solve the issues that *they* understand best, and are therefore best placed to navigate.

Second, some constraints are imposed by the organization itself, that is, *policy*. This can be understood as automated management. Managers at all levels lack the time to scrutinize every single decision that they are nominally responsible for. Instead, they set out various policies that specify what is allowed, what is not allowed and what process needs to be followed. This often applies to policies emanating from HR, IT, facilities, operations and senior management.

Since the organization imposes the policy, it can also change the policy, at least in theory. The reality is that this is often much harder than you might imagine. Rather than seek to change a policy, it is often better to ask for a specific waiver or exemption. Either way, it is important to understand that changing policy is a *political* process. This means it is necessary to identify the people that has a say in the matter and convince them of the need for the policy change or an exemption *before* you formally ask for it. This is likely to improve the chances of getting the answer you want.

Third, organizations generally exist to achieve specific *objectives*. Their resources are limited, and therefore they need to ensure that all resources ultimately contribute to their objectives. For this reason there are controls on the use of resources. These controls often take the form of budgets, head-count limits and strategic plans. The gatekeepers to resources are commonly located in functions such as accounting, finance or treasury. If you *need* resources, you will have to *ask* for it. This means demonstrating how the resources will lead to furthering the objectives of the organization. Moreover, you also need to show that your project is competitive with other potential projects in terms of how efficiently resources are converted into objectives. For profit-oriented firms, this generally amounts to demonstrating that the project is value-additive (see discussion in Chapter 12). For governmental or non-profit organizations, this requires showing that the project contributes in an efficient way to achieving the objectives of the organization.

Finally, organizations need to be aware of *social norms*. Unlike rules, compliance with social norms is generally voluntary. However, ignoring social norms might be costly. For ML projects this means paying attention to social concerns around issues such as fairness, explainability and privacy. A further nuance is that social norms are subjective and contingent. Society values both security and privacy. When these goals conflict, as they often do, there is considerable diversity of opinion as to which trade-offs are acceptable. This means it is impossible to please everyone all the time. That said, any organization has a legitimate interest in managing how it accommodates social norms. That obviously has implications for the kinds of projects that can be undertaken. For instance, while it might be legal in your jurisdiction to use ML-powered paint-guns to target repeat trespassers, it is not necessarily a good idea. Always consider the kind of headline an unsympathetic journalist might come up with. A headline such as *"Terminator bot opens fire on unarmed civilians"* is going to cause more trouble than it is worth.

In short, many of the obstacles, constraints and impediments present in organizations do serve legitimate purposes. It is also true that an unthinking reliance on rules may be an excuse for not properly exercising discretion and judgment. Either way, it is best to start engaging with these issues early in the life of a project. Often specific concerns can be addressed easily and cheaply in the design phase. It is usually much more expensive and time consuming to make big changes once the project has reached its final stages.

11.2   Governance model

A governance model sets out responsibilities and information flows. Who is responsible for delivering the project? Who is sponsoring the project? What are the milestones? and who should check progress? If the project is failing, who is responsible for stepping in and fixing things?

Most organizations have an existing governance structure. As a result, there is no need to completely reinvent the wheel. In many cases ML projects can integrate into the existing governance structure for IT projects. The key point is that an ML project requires a governance structure, just like any other activity in the organization. What does this entail? We'll sketch out an example governance structure below. Of course, this is just an example – most organizations will have their own "way of doing things" and their governance models will reflect this.

An ML project requires a *project sponsor*. Generally the sponsor will be the part of the organization that expects to benefit from the project. If the project aims to segment customers to enable better advertising campaigns, then the marketing department might be the natural sponsor. The sponsor frames the overall objectives of the project and provides the required resources (or negotiates for it to be provided).

The leadership of the project vests in the *project leader*. The project leader should be single person and not a committee. The project leader has over-all responsibility for delivering the project to the satisfaction of the project sponsor. This responsibility should be matched one-for-one with authority and resources. This role is responsible for organizing teams, allocating re-sponsibilities and resources, setting timelines and milestones, organizing re-porting, settling disputes and directly intervening if necessary. In short, the project leader is a manager, ultimately responsible for guiding the project to successful completion.

There are likely to be other parts of the organization that has a legiti-mate interest in the project, in addition to the project sponsor. These *project stakeholders* will tend to vary depending on the type of ML project, but might include the IT department (for infrastructure and policies), the legal department (for legal or compliance issues), any providers of data (opera-tions, accounting) and any other functions in the organization that have a legitimate interest in the project. Project stakeholders need to be informed on the progress and overall direction of the project, and are expected to pro-actively raise any potential issues.

The project sponsor, together with any project stakeholders, plays a su-pervisory role in relation to the project leader and project itself. This can be formalized as a *project steering committee*. The role of the project steer-ing committee is to hold the project leader accountable for delivering the project. For this reason it is advisable that the project steering committee include at least one person that is familiar with ML systems (other than the project leader). The project steering committee also provides a forum for discussing and resolving complex issues that cuts across business lines. The project steering committee advises, rather than directs, the project leader. As such it plays a similar role to a company board in relation to a CEO.

Figure 11.1 sets out an example ML project governance model. This is not the only way a governance model could be structured, and for many or-ganizations variations of Figure 11.1 might be more appropriate. In general a fit-for-purpose governance model should

1. Be clear on roles and responsibilities
2. Match responsibility with authority and resources
3. Ensure proper oversight at each level
4. Maintain a regular flow of information

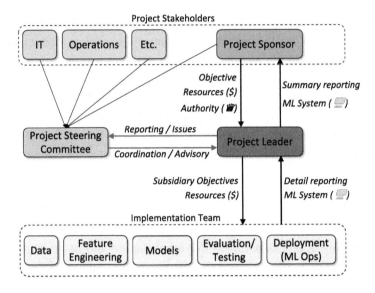

Figure 11.1 An example of an ML project governance model

11.3   Security and privacy

It is hardly necessary to stress the importance of information security in this day and age. ML systems present *threat actors* ("bad" hackers) with two targets that are valuable: data and the ability to manipulate systems.

Data is often valuable in and of itself. Financial results that have not yet been announced to the market can be used for profitable but illegal insider trading. Personal data can be sold on dark forums. Or the threat actor could encrypt your data and then demand a ransom in return for the encryption key. Since ML systems depend on data – often from many different sources and often present in bulk – they present an attractive target for threat actors.

A lesser appreciated *vulnerability* (weakness in a system) is the opportunity afforded to threat actors to manipulate or exploit decisions. Some ML systems are used to make decisions, for instance loan approvals. If a threat actor can manipulate decisions, it can force decisions that are to its own advantage but to the detriment of the organization. For instance, it could cause the loan approval system to approve a large loan to an offshore account without verified collateral in place. In practical terms, that has the same effect as having the money stolen outright. Threat actors can manipulate decisions by either attacking the system itself, or more insidiously, by providing the ML system with carefully crafted data designed to manipulate the ML system (an *adversarial data attack*).

Security for an ML system follows much the same playbook as other critical IT infrastructure.[1] Best practice in information security generally advocates that you

1. Keep your systems and software up to date (apply patches and updates regularly)
2. Switch off or disable functionality you don't need or use (minimize the *attack surface*)
3. Apply defenses at every level and within every component (the *zero-trust model*)
4. Use two-factor authentication[2] for your staff
5. Have reliable back-ups of key data and systems
6. Use encryption at the hardware and software layers

In addition you could consider

1. Operating a bounty program (pay awards to ethical hackers that point out weaknesses in your systems)
2. Employing a "Red team" to simulate an attack and probe for weaknesses
3. Running a "honey-pot" server that pretends to be your production server to misdirect (and detect) threat actors

In short, an ML project requires the same attention and care when it comes to security as any other critical organizational system.

On the other hand, adversarial data attacks are unique to ML systems and requires special care over and above the usual IT security best practice. This is mainly a problem in situations where the ML system takes input from outsiders by design, such as in the case of a loan application system. An adversarial data attack is a bit like judo, in which one ML system is used to learn how to fool another ML system. Figure 11.2 presents an adversarial attack where the addition of seemingly random noise (in fact a learned pattern) convinces the target ML system that the input image is that of a yield sign rather than a stop sign. Adversarial attacks follow the classic arms race pattern, where defenders and attackers vie for dominance. Adversarial attacks are an area of ongoing, active research, and there are no silver bullets at present. If you believe you may be vulnerable to this kind of attack you should consider getting expert advice.

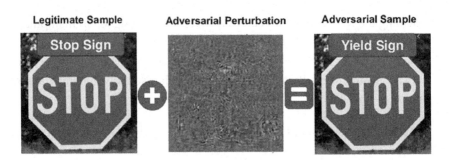

Figure 11.2 An adversarial attack on a vision system
Source: "Developing Future Human-Centered Smart Cities: Critical Analysis of Smart City Security, Interpretability, and Ethical Challenges", Figure 5. License: CC BY 4.0. Available at https://arxiv.org/abs/2012.09110

Privacy is a related concern. Privacy requires security, but security in itself does not guarantee privacy. Some types of information are particularly sensitive. Examples are medical records, financial information and political activity. One of the simplest safeguards is to only copy and use information when it is actually needed. In most ML systems, names, addresses and date of birth information is typically not needed. (You can substitute customer IDs for names, area codes for addresses and age brackets for dates of birth.)

Consent is another aspect of privacy that needs to be considered. In several jurisdictions private data may only be used for the purpose disclosed at the point of collection. This means it might be a good idea to clarify – at the point of collection – that data may be used to improve the performance of corporate activities and systems, including for training and improving internal systems. Since privacy law and regulations vary by jurisdiction, this is another area that requires specific local expertise.

11.4   Explainability and fairness

We covered *explainable AI* in some detail in Chapter 9. So why do we need to mention it again? The reason is simple. People are reluctant to accept decisions if the rationale behind it is opaque, and for good reason. ML systems *do* make mistakes, just as people do. An explainable system at least provides some hints as to what considerations drove a particular decision. In addition, explainability can greatly assist in troubleshooting ML models, both during development and in production. For this reason, some explainability should be built into the production system by design, unless there are compelling reasons not to do so (for instance, compute constraints in embedded systems).

A related issue of that is *fairness* (confusingly, sometimes referred to as bias, which should not be confused with statistical bias in predictions). A system is fair if it makes decisions only on the basis of considerations that are valid. In most advanced societies discrimination on the basis of sex, race, ethnicity, sexual orientation or religious persuasion is either illegal or at least subject to social sanction, and rightly so. I'll refer to these *potential discriminatory features* by the term *"PD features"* as a short-hand.

It follows that PD features should only be used in an ML system if there is a valid reason for doing so. To provide an example, sex or ethnicity might be relevant in certain medical settings. On the other hand, it is unclear how sex or ethnicity could be a valid basis for deciding a loan application. The straight-forward solution is to simply exclude such data from an ML system that decides loan applications.

What about features that are both valid in itself and also correlated with one or more PD features? A prime example is income. For the purposes of deciding a loan application, income is clearly a valid consideration. The ability of a borrower to service a loan *should* be considered when deciding whether to grant a loan or not. (Note that providing a loan to someone that lacks the income to service it causes harm to both the lender *and* the borrower. It does not benefit anyone.) That said, simple statistics confirm that average income often varies by sex, ethnicity and a range of other PD features. As a result, a fair loan approval system may nonetheless generate decisions that in aggregate appear to vary systematically by sex, ethnicity or other PD features. Such variation is not (necessarily) evidence of bias or unfair treatment by the loan approval system; rather it might simply reflect systematic variations in income across different groups in a particular society. The implication, as I see it, is that unequal outcomes do not *in itself* prove unequal treatment. This is not a view with universal support, by the way. Which is fine. My main point is that you and your organization should take the time to think through these issues and come up with an approach that you believe to be morally and legally defensible. Because sooner or later, you will be called on to defend what you do, and why you do it. Why not be prepared?

11.5   Laws, regulations and compliance

We have alluded to laws and regulations earlier, in particular in Section 9.1 and again in the beginning of this chapter when we discussed rules in Section 11.1. The reason for this continuing emphasis is that compliance with laws and regulations is by its very nature mandatory. You don't really have a choice. In addition, failure to adhere to laws and regulations can result in severe penalties. In financial services the financial penalties associated with non-compliance are routinely in the billions of dollars.

You should have an understanding of the relevant laws and regulations *before* you design or implement an ML system. The alternative is that you end up building a non-compliant system. In the best case you will have to rebuild it again when the non-compliance is revealed. In the worst case the non-compliance may result in expensive and time-consuming lawsuits or even criminal penalties. Simple self-interest argues for involving your legal advisers earlier rather than later.

It is tempting to summarize some of the legal requirements in the larger jurisdictions. I refrain from doing so for the following excellent reasons. First, I am not a lawyer myself, so I lack the required expertise. Second, the appropriate legal advice will invariably depend on your particular circumstances, which I am obviously not privy to. Finally, any advice I might be tempted to provide is likely to be out of date by the time you receive it. The law as applied to ML systems is rapidly evolving, just like ML itself.

In summary, take expert legal advice early, comply with it, build great ML systems and sleep well.

Notes

1   The US Cybersecurity and Infrastructure Security Agency (CISA) also provides some useful advice. Start here: https://www.cisa.gov/uscert/resources.
2   To log in, you need something you *know* (a password) and something you *have* (your phone or a special USB drive).

12 Creating value with ML

12.1 Sources of value

An organization funding an ML project will expect to benefit from it. How should we think about quantifying this value? If the organization is a profit-oriented business the objective is at least clear, so let's start there. Contrary to the business press, businesses do not generally aim to maximize their next quarter profit to the exclusion of all other concerns, and nor should they. Instead, they should aim to maximize the overall long-term value of the business while meeting the legal, regulatory and moral standards expected by society.

At least, that used to be the consensus. These days businesses are being urged to take into account ESG (environmental, social and governance) considerations alongside shareholder value. To the extent that prioritizing ESG actually boosts the overall value of the company, there is really nothing altruistic about it. Even the most cold-blooded private equity manager – with a spreadsheet where the heart should be – will gladly spend money on ESG priorities *if* the net result is to increase the value of the business.

This insight is helpful, because it means we do not need to choose between doing good and creating value when doing good *is* creating value. It amounts to the same thing. That leaves altruistic behavior that has the net effect of *reducing* the value of the firm; lets define that as *charity*.

Opinion is divided on whether private business should engage in value-destroying charity (if it does not destroy business value, then it is not charity, it is just business). One side argues that it should be left to the owners of the business – that is, the ultimate shareholders – to donate to charity, rather than

DOI: 10.4324/9781003330929-14

having the business do so for them. The other side argues that shareholders are, on the whole, too tightfisted to be counted on to donate to charity, and that therefore it is better if businesses take on that role.

Luckily, we do not need to take sides. We can simply split any organization into two conceptually distinct parts; one that maximizes value-creation and one that maximizes charitable outcomes. That split is ultimately determined via a political process involving management, shareholders, government and society.

Let's first consider value creation. Financial economists tell us that the value of a business can be determined as

$$V_t = \frac{C_{t+1}}{r - g}$$

where C_{t+1} is the expected cash flow for the next year, r is the risk-appropriate annual discount rate and g is the constant annual future growth rate in the cash flows. (This is a variation of the Gordon dividend growth model.) This makes clear the three drivers of business value: (1) next period cash flow (higher is better), (2) future growth in cash flow (higher is better) and (3) the risk-appropriate discount rate (lower is better). What does this mean for ML systems?

An ML system can add value by

- Making a one-off positive contribution to cash flow (either by increasing inflows of cash or by decreasing outflows of cash in that period): $C_{t+1} \uparrow$
- Increasing the future *growth* in cash flows, that is, increasing cash inflows or decreasing cash outflows by a certain fraction on a continuous basis: $g \uparrow$
- Reducing the *riskiness* of cash flows so that the risk-appropriate discount rate can be set at a lower rate: $r \downarrow$

In practical terms, ML systems usually contribute value by increasing the expected next period cash flow, driving future cash flow growth, or a bit of both. While reducing the riskiness of cash flows should increase firm value in theory, it might be difficult to convince people that it will do so. The reason is that there is still considerable disagreement about just how a "risk-appropriate" discount rate ought to be determined, both in industry and (especially) academia. Aiming to improve net cash flows in the short and/or long term is generally a safer bet. We'll have a bit more to say about this in Chapter 13 when we discuss drawing up a business case for an ML system.

Not all organizations exist to create value for their owners. Non-profit and governmental organizations pursue objectives that are not easily framed in dollars, and are typically funded by charitable donations or tax revenues. Given the vast actual and potential impact of these organizations on human well-being, there is every reason to help them. ML can be part of that. As in the case of profit driven organizations, spending on ML systems needs to be justifiable. Spending $50,000 on an ML system means *not* spending $50,000 on other ways of saving rain forests, curing cancer, or some other worthwhile goal. Hence the ultimate impact of the ML system needs to be quantified in terms of the goals of the organization. By way of example, a charity set up to save rain forests could use an ML system to identify patterns of deforestation from satellite images. This might lead to more effective interventions. Whether it is a good use of money depends on the next best alternative use for that money. What is the cheapest way to preserve one hectare of at-risk rain forest for one year? A charity that cares about saving rain forests should actively work at driving down that metric, while at the same time raising more money. That way the total area of saved rain forest is maximized.

12.2   The data-centric firm

Consistently generating value from ML requires more than just identifying a problem and solving it. It requires a fundamental data-first rewiring of the firm. Historically firms were organized around the need to direct specialized human labor. This typically yields hierarchical, siloed organizational structures which leaves data scattered throughout the firm in hundreds of isolated, inaccessible pockets. Most organizations don't know exactly what data they have or where it is located. (Do yours?).

Figure 12.1 presents a view of a typical industrial-era firm. The firm is organized around various functions. Each function commonly maintains their own software and database platforms to support their work. Activities that require data from different functions, such as drawing up a budget or formulating strategy, are often resource intensive because the underlying data required resides in different departmental silos. That data has to be located. Then access to the data must be negotiated, which can take days or weeks. Then the data must be extracted and standardized; again often a manual process. Finally the disparate data needs to be merged and converted into useful information to support the relevant activity. This process consists of a mix of human labor, user-maintained spreadsheets of variable quality and

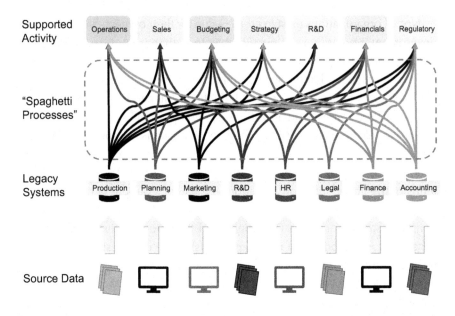

Supported
Activity

"Spaghetti
Processes"

Legacy
Systems

Source Data

Operations | Sales | Budgeting | Strategy | R&D | Financials | Regulatory

Production | Planning | Marketing | R&D | HR | Legal | Finance | Accounting

Figure 12.1 Information flow in industrial-era firms

ad-hoc script code/database queries. It is indicated in Figure 12.1 by the dashed-line box labeled "Spaghetti Processes". If you ever glance at an office building with the lights on at 6pm on a winter's evening and wonder what all those people are doing – this is what they are doing.

I would like to drive the message home with a practical example. Suppose you are tasked with forecasting sales for the next year. Sales depend on various factors – demand from clients, the firm's pricing strategy, the price response from competitors, production and transportation costs, general economic conditions and so forth. You will need to obtain data from the Accounting, Operations, Planning and Distribution departments and perhaps a few more. For each you will need to find the right people, schedule time for a call to explain what you need and why, understand what data they have, how it is structured and how it can be accessed. The departments might be hesitant to share data, often citing security or privacy issues (some of which may even be real). Once that is resolved, you will need to obtain the right kind of system privileges to access the data, set up connections to various kinds of databases/repositories, download data – and clean up user-supplied spreadsheets for the departments that don't use databases. It could easily take a week or two to get this far. Only then can you combine and clean the data, build a model and produce the sales forecast. From your perspective the whole process is painful, inefficient and slow. But from the perspective of the departments involved, they are simply doing their job and following standard procedures. Many people in the organization might not even understand why you are unhappy. After all, you get paid by the hour, just like everybody else, so why complain?

In summary, the industrial-era structure makes it difficult, expensive and time consuming to build any kind of system that depends on data from across the organization. And ML systems require data, first and foremost. You *can* build ML systems within this structure, but the expected benefit will need to be very high to justify the equally high cost and effort required.

In Figure 12.2 we present an alternative architecture that is better suited to the data-centric era. The core idea is to provide a centrally maintained enterprise data repository that can be accessed via a common data interface. Such a repository consists of more than just dumping all your data on a beefy server. A properly structured data repository should enforce standard security protocols, ensure privacy, maintain versioning and keep audit logs. Because there is only one repository, the firm can and should invest in automating these controls. The net result is simplicity. There is a single

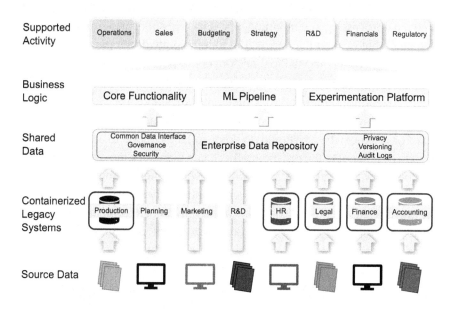

Figure 12.2 Information flow in data-centric firms

source of data that can be accessed using a single data interface. Returning to our earlier example, you might be able to source the data you need in an afternoon, rather than spending weeks on it. That means the sales forecast can be delivered by Friday, rather than the end of next month.

This level of integration and automation is the premise of so-called *enterprise resource planning* (ERP) software. ERP vendors such as SAP, Oracle and Microsoft offer software suites that support typical business activities such as supply chain management, HR, financial reporting and so on. For an organization that doesn't need anything else, a well-configured ERP system may well be a sensible solution. Since all ERP systems are built on top of an integrated database, it is simply a matter of making that data available for use in ML systems as needed. However, for many large organizations the standard ERP offerings doesn't meet all of their software requirements. In those cases the ERP system is just one part of the overall software ecosystem, and the rationale for setting up an Enterprise Data Repository remains intact.

The enterprise data repository supports core functionality required to run the firm and make decisions. In an ideal world, much of what is currently done manually in spreadsheets could be converted into production quality code that just works without any human involvement. Cutting and pasting data between spreadsheets is tedious and error-prone. While spreadsheets are excellent for *ad-hoc* analysis, they are generally not well suited to routine data processing and reporting. The data repository also supports the ML Pipeline, that is, shared infrastructure for efficiently developing ML systems. Chapter 14 covers the ML Pipeline concept in detail.

Finally, the data repository can support experimentation. Some organizations have an opportunity to try different things and see what works best. Doing this well requires experiments. A very common approach is *A/B testing*. For instance, the firm could randomly offer a coupon to a few customers (group A) and not to the rest (group B).[1] It can then track the overall profit per customer for both group A and group B over the next month. If the overall profit per customer in group A is significantly higher than group B, it could be worthwhile rolling out the offer to the remaining customers in group B. If not, the amount of money lost on group A will be modest since only a relatively small number of customers were allocated to group A. A similar approach could be used to evaluate whether a new ML system is better than the system it replaces. Tracking experiments manually can be time-consuming and error-prone, so it makes sense to automate it and integrate it with the enterprise data repository.

The reality is that most firms cannot simply dispense with their existing core systems (production scheduling, accounting, payroll and so on). Figure 12.2 shows how these systems can be accommodated in the new architecture. Every supplier of data (e.g. legacy systems or raw data sources) provide data only to the enterprise data repository. Every user of data must source that data only from the enterprise data repository. This greatly reduces the number of data connections and the associated costs and risk. If you have 50 suppliers of data and 300 users of data, the "spaghetti process" in Figure 12.1 could grow to $50 \times 300 = 15,000$ distinct data flows, each with their own unique set of interface issues, privacy concerns, security implications and governance considerations. By contrast, the architecture in Figure 12.2 requires at most $50 + 300 = 350$ distinct data flows – a roughly 40-fold reduction compared to Figure 12.1. Moreover, the approach in Figure 12.2 ensures a consistent approach to issues of governance, security, privacy, audit controls and versioning. Should any of those require changes, it is straightforward to implement it in one place and have the changes apply globally.

Setting up the architecture presented in Figure 12.2 will itself require a considerable investment. In return for this substantial fixed investment, the firm gains a significant reduction in the cost and time required to stand up new data-driven functionality, including those that make use of ML. In this sense it presents the classic choice between high fixed costs but low marginal costs on the one hand, and low fixed costs but high marginal costs on the other. The purpose of Figure 12.2 is to illustrate a key idea: an investment in shared data infrastructure lowers the cost of data-driven innovation. As such it should not be taken as a one-size-fits-all blueprint. If your organization is only ever going to implement one ML system, there may be cheaper and more effective ways to make that happen. On the other hand, if your organization is likely to commission a dozen or so ML systems each year, an architecture similar to that of Figure 12.2 becomes a compelling proposition.

12.3 The economics of platforms

When you remove *all* human involvement from a workflow, something interesting happens – the marginal cost of processing another unit drops to something close to zero.[2] Consider the world before the internet and search engines. If you lacked a particular piece of information, you had to expend time and effort to locate it. This might involve checking any books or articles you had to hand, manually scanning for the information, of perhaps taking a trip to a library or a bookstore. In fact, finding information was often a paid position with the title of "research assistant" or similar. Locating a crucial but obscure bit of information could take hours or days, in the process costing somewhere between a nice dinner and a nice holiday. Today you type your question – however obscure – into a search engine and that is it. The *marginal* cost of processing a search request is likely less than a cent. By constructing and maintaining a vast infrastructure companies like Google have been able to completely automate the workflow of processing a search query.

This is an extreme example of *economies of scale*. By investing up-front a firm can lower the marginal cost of producing each unit. Once a sufficient volume is produced the total cost per unit can be much lower than that of a competitor that had forgone the up-front investment and is therefore stuck with a high marginal cost.

When you can do something valuable very cheaply, you have an opportunity to construct entirely new business models, as Google illustrated by building an advertising business around search results. The value of ML lies in its ability to automate processes that used to require human input, thereby driving marginal unit cost toward zero. It is no accident that Google refers to itself as an "AI company" and invests billions of dollars in AI research and infrastructure. The same is true of other *platform companies* such as Apple or Facebook.

That is only the cost side. Now consider the value side. Some products benefit from so-called *network effects*. This means that each additional customer increases the value experienced by every existing customer. Social media is the prime example. To be useful, a social media app should have people on it; the more the better. And the higher the value, the more opportunities there are to monetize the business. With network effects, the total value created grows faster than the volume of users.

The final consideration is data. Data is the raw material from which ML systems are fashioned. That makes data intrinsically valuable. When you are able to grow the volume you are processing, you are also generating new data that can fuel further improvements in algorithms and support new products and businesses. We can refer to this as *data effects*.

To summarize, platform companies exploit economies of scale, network effects and data effects to create value that grows faster than volume.

Figure 12.3 provides a graphical illustration of these effects. Consider a business, which we will call a "studio", that has zero fixed costs. Every unit it

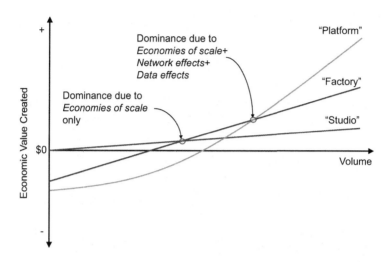

Figure 12.3 Value vs volume – studios, factories and platforms

produces consumes a fixed cost and generates a fixed economic value. As a result the profit per unit is constant, irrespective of the volume produced. At a volume of zero, the studio generates zero value. The amount of value created by the studio for a given volume of production is depicted by the straight line labeled "Studio" in Figure 12.3. If this seems quaint and contrived, it is worth remembering that this was the dominant mode of production prior to the industrial revolution.

Let's introduce a new kind of business that we will call a "factory". A factory requires a large up-front investment. However, thereafter it can produce units at a much lower marginal cost. At a volume of zero the value created is negative, reflecting the expenditure of the up-front investment. The line labeled "factory" in Figure 12.3 plots value versus volume for a factory business. When volume grows sufficiently large, the value created by a factory surpasses that of a studio. In other words, a factory benefits from economies of scale. This is the mode of production that powered the industrial revolution. Factories is why you can buy a new bicycle for the price of a yoga session.

Finally, a platform is a business that benefits not only from economies of scale, but also from network effects and data effects. The curved line in Figure 12.3 plots the value/volume relationship for a platform. If sufficiently powerful, the network and data effects can supercharge the relationship between value and volume so that a 10% increase in volume leads to an increase in value exceeding 10%. This is what generates the positive curvature in the platform line. Platform companies are dominating the information age. (Have another look at Table 1.1 in Chapter 1 if you need to be convinced.)

How do you survive direct competition with a platform company if you are a factory or studio business yourself? Simply slugging it out on their terms is probably not the best course of action. Platform companies with dominant positions are very powerful competitors, with access to huge amounts of accumulated data, significant compute resources, vast internal talent and a few billion dollars of revenue coming in the door every quarter. In the short run the only viable competitor to a platform company is another platform company. It is no accident that the competitors to AWS (the cloud computing arm of Amazon) are Google (GCP) and Microsoft (Azure), both established platform companies themselves (in search and software, respectively). However, in the longer run even the platform giants are vulnerable to rapid changes in technology and consumer preferences. Two ways of surviving competition from a platform is specialization and augmentation. A *specialization strategy* entails serving a smaller but profitable market whose needs are not met by the "one size fits all" offerings from platform companies. An *augmentation strategy* provides products or services that are complementary to those of platform companies. So rather than fighting the platform company you ride their coattails. Finally, you could build out a platform business yourself. (If you are tempted to do so, I highly recommend that you consult "*Competing in the Age of AI: Strategy and Leadership When Algorithms and Networks Run the World*", by Marco Iansiti and Karim Lakhani. This chapter draws on many of their insights.)

12.4   Outside of platforms

A competitive advantage depends on having something that your competitors do not have. But if you can use ML, then so can your competitors. In theory identical firms end up in identical places. But in practice firms are never really identical. Even small differences in quality and speed of execution can put some ahead of others, often permanently. In many markets the existence of economies of scale, along with network and data effects, almost guarantees that there will emerge a handful of dominant firms along with a plethora of imitators and niche players.

In other markets economies of scale, network effects and data effects might by less important. In these markets one would expect competition along value and quality dimensions to be intense – think of coffee shops. How, exactly, would you use ML to run a coffee shop better? (This is a good interview question!) Coffee shops are particularly resistant to automation, mainly because people happen to like buying coffee from people, not machines. There *are* things you could do. Demand prediction for instance. In the same way we predicted traffic flows in Chapter 4 you could attempt to predict the volume of sales each day. With good demand predictions you can improve the scheduling of staff, inventory levels and so forth. This is probably not worth doing for a single coffee shop, but it probably *is* worth doing for a large chain of coffee shops (they might do this already). It might also be worth doing if you are a supplier of coffee to independent coffee shops. You can offer this as a free service in exchange for real-time data on sales. You can then use this information to improve your *own* demand forecasts. It also makes the independent coffee shops less likely to switch to an alternative supplier for a slightly better price.

The moral – if you can't think of a way to use ML to solve your own problems, ask yourself whether you can solve your *customer's* problems. Sometimes a supplier may be better placed to solve a problem with ML than the customer, since the supplier can amortize the required investment across thousands of customers, something the customers themselves cannot easily do.

Notes

1 The "randomly" part is really important because it means the *intervention* (also referred to as a *treatment* or *experiment* in some contexts) is the only systematic difference between the groups, and therefore any significant difference in outcomes between the groups can be directly attributed to the intervention. If the intervention is not random, it is difficult to be sure that the intervention, rather than other differences between the groups, caused the outcome. This problem is well understood in econometrics – see https://en.wikipedia.org/wiki/Endogeneity_(econometrics) and Roberts and Whited (2013) [https://papers.ssrn.com/sol3/papers.cfm?abstract_id=1748604].
2 Marginal cost is a term from micro-economics. It means the extra cost of producing one additional unit.

13 Making the business case

You will need to convince people in your organization to support an ML project. In general, the hurdles to obtaining approval will be proportional to the resources you require, which in turn will grow with the scope and ambition of the project. For the purposes of this chapter we will assume that the project is significant in scope, with commensurately large resource requirements.

How do you convince your organization that a particular project should get the go-ahead? The overarching insight is that you need to appeal to priorities of the organization, or perhaps more cynically, to the priorities of the ultimate decision makers in the organization. It follows that the first steps should include understanding (a) what the priorities of the organization are, (b) who the decision makers are and (c) what the priorities and constraints faced by the decision makers are.

We can normally take it for granted that a profit-oriented business will show an interest in anything that can reduce costs or increase revenue, after accounting for the likely expense involved. There will be preference for projects that are simple, quick, and with low execution risk and high expected benefits.

In government and non-profit organizations cost savings are likely to find support, as are ways to achieve the organization's aims more effectively, more efficiently, or both. Organizations of all stripes are likely to show an interest in projects that can materially reduce risk for a small outlay, especially large risks that can put the organization itself (or its senior management) at risk. This is commonly viewed as akin to buying insurance.

It may not be obvious, but senior decision makers are in practice constrained in terms of what they can approve. Even CEOs are accountable for

DOI: 10.4324/9781003330929-15

their decisions. In other words, decision makers understand that they may be asked in the future to explain why they made a particular decision. Keep in mind that even good decisions sometimes result in bad outcomes due to bad luck. In those cases decision makers will need to be able to back up their decisions by showing that, given what was known at the time, the decision was a sensible one. It is also difficult for decision makers to approve a project when they receive advice to the contrary from specialist functions such as IT or compliance. In practice, this means that you may need to convince not only the decision maker, but also those other stakeholders whose views could influence the decision maker.

To summarize, these following are questions that need answers *before* you sit down to write a business case:

1. What do you propose?
2. How will it benefit the organization?
3. What resources are required?
4. Who will do it?
5. Who are the decision maker(s)?
6. Who are potential stakeholders?
7. What are the incentives and constraints of decision makers and stakeholders?

The answers above will help you decide whether the project is organizationally feasible. That is to say, can it be done? And more specifically, can it be done by *your* organization? A proposal should at least be possible in theory (point 1), be expected to benefit the organization (point 2), require no more resources than the organization can spare (point 3), be implemented using available talent (point 4), and finally, be palatable to senior decision maker(s) and any potential stakeholders (points 6 and 7).

Once you have convinced yourself that the project is feasible and will benefit the organization, it is time to convince other people. This does not necessarily require a written *business case* (also known as a *project proposal*). However, it is a good idea to have it written down. The discipline of writing things down can help clarify your thinking. It also makes it easier to circulate the idea within the organization. Finally, a written business case makes it more likely that everyone shares the same understanding of what is proposed.

So how should you write a business case? There is no one "right" way to structure a business case, just as there is no one right way to write a novel or construct a model. Instead, a well-written business case should be persuasive. One way to approach this is to anticipate the questions a decision maker might ask about the project. The list below covers some of the questions that tends to be asked, along with possible section headers in a business case.

- *Just cut to the chase* – Executive summary
- *What do you want to do?* – Description of the project
- *Why should we do it?* – Project benefits
- *Can it even be done?* – Proof-of-concept (pilot project)
- *How much will it cost?* – Required resources
- *How are you going to do it?* – Technical appendix

I'll briefly discuss each of these headings.

13.1 Executive summary

The executive summary is the only part of the business case that you can count on to be read with care and attention. It is therefore important that it explains what is being proposed and why it is a good idea in clear, simple terms. The total length of the executive summary should not exceed three pages; but a single page is better if you can manage it.

If the executive summary is the only part that most people will read, why should you bother with the other 27 pages? First, there may be *some* people that will read the entire business case. Both the project sponsor and the project lead need to be familiar with the detail of the business case, since it serves to document the scope and objectives of the project. Second, while most people will not read the entire business case, they will nonetheless want to see that *someone else* has taken the time and effort to think through the details. A detailed, well-presented business case suggests the existence of a detailed, well-considered plan. Conversely, a vague and cursory business plan does not tend to inspire confidence. The truth is that appearances *do* matter. So, of course, does substance. But in practice appearance precedes substance. As a result you might only get the opportunity to demonstrate substance if the appearance inspires sufficient confidence to get the go-ahead on a project.

13.2   Description of the project

This section describes what the project is setting out to achieve. This includes both the ML task to be solved, and a brief non-technical discussion of how the problem might be solved. The second part is necessarily provisional, since part of the project consists of finding the best way to solve the task at hand. Nonetheless, it is generally helpful if you can show that you have some idea of how to approach the problem. The discussion should be kept non-technical; the more technical aspects of the proposal can be relegated to an appendix.

Ideally a description of the project will cover the following ground:

- The problem that is being solved from the organization's perspective
- A description of how the task is currently accomplished (if that is the case)
- How the problem can be framed as an ML task (and why that would be an improvement, if that is the case)
- If it is a supervised task, a description of the target variable
- A description of the data required to train the model
- The key performance metrics to be used to evaluate the system
- The minimum performance level at which the project is viable

In addition, the business case should set out who is sponsoring the project (the project sponsor) and who has ultimate responsibility for delivering the project (the project leader).

13.3   Project benefits

The business case needs to explain how the project will benefit the organization. The most convincing way to do this is to relate the problem being solved to aims of the organization. If your organization is a business, its primarily aim is to make money. It can be helpful to start with the objective of the organization, show it how relates to a particular task or problem, before explaining how an ML system can solve that task or problem better. Here is an example in the context of a physical security provider:

- Sentinel Security LLC[1] aims to generate returns for our shareholders by delivering a valuable service to our customers (copied straight from last year's annual report)

127

- One of our services is the provision of intrusion detection services to industrial customers (ditto)
- We currently provide this service using a mixture of on-site security personnel and recorded security cameras
- Security personnel are expensive to deploy, while security cameras do not provide real-time alerts, which is particularly valued by our customers
- We propose to create an ML algorithm to detect suspicious activity from security camera feeds and provide real-time, actionable alerts
- We expect the deployment of such a system to improve our incident detection rate from 83% to around 97%, thus providing a significant boost to the value we provide to customers
- In addition, on-site personnel requirements will be reduced by between 20% and 50%, which amounts to a significant reduction in costs
- Net of expected development and deployment costs, the project is expected to improve net profit by $11.2 million per annum (an increase of 8%)

Note the quantification of benefits in dollars terms in the last point. Expect to be challenged on any hard numbers you provide. It goes without saying that those numbers need to be backed up with a detailed spreadsheet based on reasonable assumptions. In which case you should be fine. If the only argument is about whether the positive profit impact is $11.2 million or in fact only $8.6 million, the project is going to get the go-ahead either way.

Something that can be quite helpful is to explicitly link a measure of ML performance to a measure of business performance. For instance, one could create a plot of improvement in annual profit as a function of the accuracy of a particular model. Figure 13.1 provides an example where the increase in profit is plotted against model accuracy for a central estimate, along with a conservative and optimistic scenario. According to Figure 13.1 achieving the target accuracy of 89% should yield an increase in profit per annum of just over $4 million. The graphs demonstrates visually that there is little to be gained by pushing accuracy much beyond 90%. Analysis such as that of Figure 13.1 can avoid spending thousands of dollars trying to push model performance beyond where it matters for the business. While the numbers in Figure 13.1 are made-up, an attempt should be made to link model performance with business outcomes. This is not always straight-forward, since it can be difficult to estimate the business impact of a particular performance

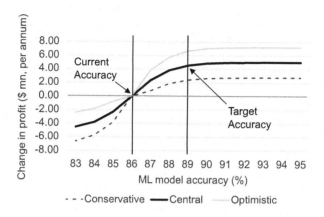

Figure 13.1 Improvement in profit as a function of model accuracy

level. The utility of this exercise is that it can serve as guide to how much effort should be expended on model performance.

13.4 Proof-of-concept

For an organization that lacks substantial experience in developing and deploying ML systems, the prospect of doing so can seem risky. The same is true when applying ML in new and unfamiliar problem domains. In such cases it may be prudent to build a proof-of-concept system as part of the process. The benefit of building a proof-of-concept system is that it can resolve a lot of the uncertainties and risks at a relatively low cost. This is appealing to organizations. If you can't steer, then it is comforting to at least have your foot poised over the brakes. A proof-of-concept system provides the organization with the opportunity to re-assess its commitment to the project once it has much better information regarding the feasibility of the proposed system and its likely ability to contribute value to the organization.

It can be quite hard to get sign-off to spend a couple of million dollars on a novel technology with an uncertain payoff, even if that payoff could be in the millions. By comparison it is straight-forward to get approval to spend $50,000 on a pilot project that might open the door to millions in value – and if not, the $50,000 is a bargain if it avoids spending millions on a system that has no hope of making back the investment.

In building out a proof-of-concept, the goal is *not* to build a robust, high quality ML system. Instead, the goal is to learn as quickly as possible whether building a system with the required performance is even possible. As a result, you can and should take short-cuts. In the end you will throw away the proof-of-concept system – and retain the valuable information learned. Once you have sufficient data in place, it is often possible to build out half a dozen different models in a few minutes to a few days. If you are able to iterate quickly toward performance numbers that approach (or even exceed) the minimum viable level, it provides assurance that the full-scale production system should be able to also meet those performance requirements. This removes a very significant part of the project risk. Other risks remain, such as building robust pipelines, reliable error reporting and ensuring security. However, these engineering-type risks are typically better understood and easier to manage than fundamental doubt about the ability of machine learning systems to solve a particular task.

A successful proof-of-concept essentially de-risks an ML project in terms of technical feasibility. This, in turn, makes it much more likely that the organization will commit the resources required to build out a full-scale production system.

13.5   Required resources

To be able to quantify the net benefits of undertaking the project it is necessary to first quantify the costs. These costs normally entail staff time, access to data and compute resources. Which means money; with sufficient funds, it is possible to hire staff, buy data and pay for computers. The staffing side requires careful consideration. If you lack all of the required talent in-house, it will be necessary to hire from outside the firm. In most instances this will take some time; at least a few weeks but possibly a few months (the staff you hire may have to serve out notice periods). Alternatively you may be able to engage consultants for those roles. This is quicker, but also more expensive. These considerations should be factored into the business plan.

13.6   Technical appendix

Any technical material should be relegated to a technical appendix. Technical matters are important, but not everyone needs to (or wants to) know. If something involves equations (loss functions or performance measures) or references specific tools or frameworks (e.g. Tensorflow), it is a good candidate for the technical appendix. At this point, you might question why it is even necessary to have a technical appendix. The answer is that when you present a business case, you are in a sense asserting that what you are proposing to do can in fact be done. Sketching out some of the technical considerations shows that you understand the problem to be solved at the technical level, and you at least have some ideas about how to engineer a solution. Naturally the system when finally completed may look very different from the approach sketched out initially. But a complete lack of technical details suggest that no one has taken the time to think things through, and this is not an encouraging sign.

What information should be in the technical appendix? To a large extent this will depend on the problem domain and the chosen ML approach, but the following is a useful starting point:

1. Formal statement of the ML task (even better if it can be written as a mathematical statement)

2. If a supervised learning problem

    (a) The target variable

    (b) A description of the potential features (e.g. accounting data, customer reviews, etc.)

    (c) Regression task (predict a number) or classification task (predict a class)

    (d) ML approach (or approaches) to consider

    (e) Loss function used for each approach

    (f) List of performance measures for evaluating performance

3. If an unsupervised learning problem

    (a) The nature of the problem (e.g. dimensionality reduction or clustering)

    (b) The ML approach (or approaches) to consider

    (c) The objective (what is being minimized or maximized)

    (d) Performance measures (how can you differentiate between a good solution and a bad solution?)

4. Hyper-parameter optimization

(a) Which hyper-parameters (and if numeric, over which range)

(b) The criteria for choosing the best hyper parameter (it doesn't *have* to be the same as the loss function)

5. A description of the data

   (a) Likely number of columns (usually features)

   (b) Likely number of rows (usually instances)

   (c) Approach for splitting the data into training, validation and test sets

6. Any data preprocessing steps that are required

   (a) Data cleaning and validation

   (b) Imputing missing values

   (c) Scaling or standardization

   (d) Dimensionality reduction

7. Computing resources required

   (a) Memory (RAM)

   (b) Storage (Disk space)

   (c) CPU or CPU+GPU?

   (d) Single machine or multiple machines?

   (e) In-house or cloud computing provider?

8. List of required software packages or frameworks (including version numbers!)

If you are able to address the points above, it demonstrates that you have a good understanding of what is required from a technical point of view.

I emphasize again that the best business case is one that persuades decision makers because it correctly anticipates their questions, and provides clear, convincing answers to those questions. As a result the ideal structure and content of a business case depends on what is needed to achieve that, rather than just following some fixed formula.

Note

1   Sentinel Security LLC is an invention of my own. Any resemblance to real security providers is entirely coincidental.

14 The ML pipeline

14.1 Who needs a pipeline anyway?

The business case has been approved. A pilot project demonstrated the feasibility of building a model with the required performance. Now what? Perhaps you should organize a team dinner to celebrate, pausing only to email the pilot project – all 168 lines of Python code – to IT with a request to put it into production? Not so fast. Keep in mind the discussion in Chapter 11. Can you show that the ML model is fully secure, preserves privacy, is compliant with all rules and regulations, can seamlessly scale to handle demand 1,000× greater than tested in the pilot project, is demonstrably fair and unbiased, can be explained when needed, evaluates its own performance continuously *and* has full audit trails of both code and data? I guess not. Also, how much potential performance are you giving up by not carefully exploring all possible avenues for improving performance? What does this mean in terms of dollars not earned or not saved?

This unkind line of questioning reveals a general truth. Building a working pilot model is the start, not the end, of the work required to build a production-ready ML system.

When building an ML system we make a distinction between building the ML pipeline and developing the ML model. An ML pipeline is a prerequisite for developing any but the most trivial ML systems. In addition, a well-structured ML pipeline can be reused for subsequent ML projects, so it is worth building it properly the first time.

So, what is an ML pipeline exactly? Simply stated an *ML pipeline* is software that automates all of the steps required to go from raw data to a trained model. The term pipeline is apt, since the natural way to structure an ML

DOI: 10.4324/9781003330929-16

project is as a sequence of processes. Each process takes the output from the previous process, does something to it, and passes it on to the next process. The initial input into the pipeline is the raw data on which the model is to be trained and evaluated. The final output from the pipeline is a trained model, along with a set of performance measures that reflects the ability of the trained model.

The automated nature of the pipeline is essential. Applied ML is still largely an empirical process. The only reliable way to know if a change will improve performance is to try it out on the validation data. It follows that there is a lot of "trying out" involved in getting the best performance out of ML. Unless the process of trying out something different is automated, the model development process will quickly grind to a halt.

Consider a practical example. Imagine that a demand forecast model produces errors that are much higher when it rains. The likely reason is that weather plays some role in determining demand. (Perhaps you are modeling ice-cream sales in a park or beer sales in a pub garden.) Thus the forecasted weather should be included as a feature. With a fully automated ML pipeline this is relatively straight-forward – download historical weather predictions, add it to the raw data store and add the weather feature to the list of features to be used. Then click "run", clear a few emails, and check if the new model improved performance on the validation data.[1] This is not something you will do a just a handful of times. If the pipeline takes few minutes to run end-to-end (a realistic estimate with hundreds of features and millions of instances) you might easily do this hundreds of times over the course of a few of weeks of model development. To iterate efficiently through different ideas during model development you really have no choice but to rely on an automated ML pipeline.

These days there are several good ML frameworks that make it relatively simple to build an ML pipeline. The major cloud computing providers all have services for hosting machine learning systems, and often one can stitch together a basic ML pipeline with a few clicks. Despite this, it is important to understand the motivation behind ML pipelines.

14.2 The ML pipeline

Figure 14.1 depicts an example ML pipeline.

In Figure 14.1 the process starts at the bottom with the raw data. We are assuming here that all the required data are available from an enterprise data

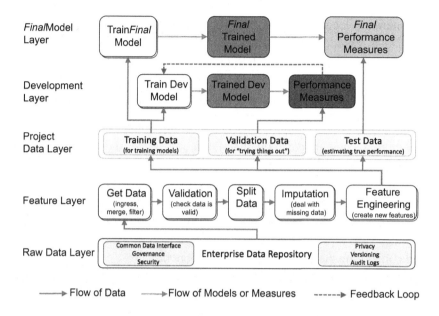

Figure 14.1 An example of an ML pipeline

repository, following best practice (also see Figure 12.2). This is followed by the feature layer. This layer processes the data so that it is ready to be used to train an ML model. Note that the "Split Data" step precedes imputation and feature engineering – this is to prevent accidental data leakage between the training, validation and test data sets. Because the steps are sequential, and each step only depends on the output of the previous step, it should be simple to add or remove steps. For instance, we could add a "Scaling" step after the "Feature Engineering" to prepare the data for a neural network model. Similarly, we could remove the "Imputation" step if the model we are using can handle missing data internally, as is the case with gradient boosting machine models, for example.

To summarize, an ML pipeline automates the process of going from raw data to a trained model. To be useful the ML pipeline needs to be automated, which in practical terms means that everything is done with software. There should be no manual steps. (If anything needs to be done differently, then it should be done by changing the pipeline code.)

The benefits of an ML pipeline are

- Less effort to build new models or tweak existing models
- Much faster to iterate through different ideas

- Automatic logging of data, models and performance measures (which enables reproducibility)
- Enforces a standard approach to model construction
- Enables the reuse of modules
- Automates testing, logging, versioning and reporting

Surely there must be some drawbacks to using an ML pipeline? Yes, there are. Putting together an ML pipeline takes time, effort and resources. If you build out your own pipeline, that takes time. If you use an established pipeline framework, you will still need to spend time to understand how that framework functions and how to adapt it to the ML model you are developing. The same goes for structuring ML pipelines in the cloud. While you may save time on coding, you will still need to spend time setting up and configuring the various pipeline components.

Perhaps one of the bigger challenges is explaining to stakeholders why you are spending time building out a pipeline when the pilot project already constitutes an ML model with acceptable performance. The short answer is that an ML pipeline is a prerequisite to realizing the full potential of ML. The first model is rarely the best model. But without an ML pipeline you won't get much beyond the first model.

Note

1   Remember, never "try things out" on the test data. That is what the validation data is for. Test data is for testing the *final* model, and nothing else.

15 Development

15.1 A very brief introduction to software engineering

An ML system *is* software. Hence the accumulated experience of building software systems is directly relevant to building ML systems. Since the dawn of the computer age in the 1960's we have learned a few things about building reliable software. Insofar as it is relevant to building ML systems, I present a few of the high-level insights gained. What follows is a *very* brief and selective introduction to best practices in software engineering.

15.1.1 Divide and conquer

Most software tasks are far too complex to just sit down and write code. Consider the complexity involved in writing a browser or a database system from scratch. Instead, the tried and tested approach is to create software by breaking each task into simpler sub-tasks until you arrive at tasks that are simple enough to solve directly with computer code. These solved low-level tasks then become the building blocks for solving the higher-level tasks until eventually the whole task is solved.

In the context of an ML system, we could start by to dividing the system into logically coherent sub-units (*modules*) such as data acquisition, data validation, missing data imputation, feature construction, hyper-parameter tuning, model training, and model evaluation. "Missing data imputation" is still a complex task, but it is substantially less complex than implementing an entire machine learning system. We can keep decomposing the missing data imputation module into simpler tasks – for instance imputing missing

DOI: 10.4324/9781003330929-17

values for a single variable using a specific approach, such as replacing missing values with zero. At this point the task is simple enough to implement directly in code. If you keep doing this, eventually all tasks are converted into code and the original task is solved.

15.1.2 Expose interfaces, hide implementations

Each module should expose an *interface*, that is, a clearly defined way to interact with the module. The interface is for telling the module *what* to do, but crucially, not *how* to do it. The how-to part (the *implementation*) remains internal to the module, so we don't need to worry about it when we interact with the module. This is something you have already seen. An ML model is an example of a module. At a conceptual level, there are two things a model should be able to do – train itself, and once trained, make predictions. The interface for a model consists of `model.train(X, y)` for training, and `y = model.predict(X)` for prediction. When we use the interface, we ignore all of the complexity that goes into actually training a model or making model predictions, which can be considerable. This is an example of *abstraction* – revealing only what we need to know while hiding everything else. When multiple implementations share the same interface, it is straight-forward to change from one implementation to another without affecting the rest of the system. For example, if we want to change from a `LinearRegression` model to a `DecisionTreeRegressor` model, all we need to do is replace `model = LinearRegression(...)` in our code with `model = DecisionTreeRegression(...)`. The rest of the code does not need to change, since both LinearRegression and DecisionTreeRegressor support training and predicting using the *same* interface – `model.train(X, y)` and `y = model.predict(X)`. This is possible because our code only tells the model *what* to do (e.g. training or predicting) and leaves it up to the model implementation to handle the internal details of *how* to do it.

If this seems a bit abstract, it might help to consider that large organizations operate in a very similar fashion. Most organizations are also organized in a hierarchy, just like software systems. Within that hierarchy different business units expose interfaces ("to take annual leave, lodge a leave request in the HR system" or "process a refund for client transaction 003420043") while hiding the actual implementation.

Accumulated experience suggests that software engineering works best when we construct software systems from internally coherent modules that interact only via clearly specified interfaces. With such an architecture, complexity is limited to that which is directly relevant to the particular task or context. This makes it much easier to understand the behavior of the system, and to modify or extend it if needed.

15.1.3   Implement incrementally

When it comes to implementation, historically there has been two competing approaches. The first, often referred to as the "big-bang" approach, entails building the entire system exactly as specified. Once constructed in full, work moves to identifying and fixing any remaining issues before deploying the system in production. The second approach is incremental, with additional functionality added to the system only when testing confirms that all current issues have been addressed; this is sometimes referred to as the "agile" approach.

In the foregoing I say "historically", since these days you will struggle to find many supporters of the big-bang approach, at least among experienced developers. The reason is that when the time comes to test and deploy a big-bang developed system, there is typically an avalanche of problems, issues and bugs. Fixing these problems are hard for three reasons. First, the problems could be due to mistakes *anywhere* in the code (which may number hundreds of thousands of lines of code). This makes it difficult to find bugs. Second, it is hard to test a system that already has multiple issues, since unrelated issues may prevent you from even running the code you would like to test. Third, it is difficult to know if a particular fix is effective, since any remaining problematic behavior could be due to any of the dozens of other bugs still present in the code. It may well be quicker to write software using the big-bang approach, but the weeks of development time saved will be lost during the subsequent months spent chasing down and fixing a seemingly never-ending list of problems.

Incremental software development starts with a system that operates correctly, even if the implemented functionality is minimal. (The very first iteration might simply print a copyright notice and then terminate.) Thereafter functionality is added to the system incrementally. Each time functionality is added, the system is tested to ensure that both the new and previous functionality operates correctly. (Much of this testing can be automated; this is considered best practice). As a result, at each point during development there is a version of the system that is known to operate correctly. When an issue crops up after adding new functionality, it is generally much easier to find the cause of the problem. In most cases, the problem is caused by one of the hundred or so lines of code that implement the new functionality. Second, there are usually no more than a handful of new problems that crop up in each iteration. This makes it much easier to verify that a particular fix actually solves the problem, since there is high confidence that the rest of the system operates correctly. As a result, the end point of each iteration is a stable, tested system that works properly. This means that when the last bit of functionality is successfully added to the system, the system is both complete *and correct*.

15.1.4   *Use version control*

Version control is simply the ability to record historical changes in the source code making up a software project. Crucially, this includes the ability to re-vert the code to earlier state (e.g. when it was working correctly, *before* making a series of disastrous changes). For a single developer working alone version control is helpful and occasionally a lifesaver. For a team of developers, version control is crucial. For a distributed team of developers, version control is quite simply indispensable. A real-world example is the source code for *Linux*, an open-source operating system. The source code for Linux is hosted on github.com, a cloud-based distributed version control system, and is the product of more than 13 *thousand* contributors.[1]

In an organizational setting version control provides a practical way to manage and track changes to production code. This is essential for security and reliability. In the context of machine learning systems, version control makes it possible to identify and record the exact code used to generate a specific model.

15.1.5   *Conduct automated testing*

It is embarrassingly easy introduce a bug when adding new code, or – especially – when making changes to existing code. There are two types of testing that can help catch bugs early (and early is the best possible time to catch a bug). The first is termed *unit testing*; essentially it amounts to checking that newly coded functionality works correctly. Ideally, this should happen before the code is merged back into the version control system. Often the programmer writing the new code is also the person that performs the unit testing.

The other kind of testing is *regression testing*, which is just a fancy term for re-testing all the existing code after making changes to any one part of the code. These tests usually cover both individual bits of functionality as well as overall functionality. That is, it checks for the correctness of both individual components and the correct functioning of the overall system. In most large projects regression testing is automated; in a typical workflow the tests are run overnight after all the code changes for the day has been committed to the version control system.

It is important to stress that an absence of test errors does not prove correctness (the absence of bugs). However, the presence of test errors does prove the existence of at least one bug. While a known bug is bad, an unknown bug is much, much worse. In this sense automated testing provides a fallible, but still very valuable, safety net.

15.2 Validating the pipeline

A good starting point is to build confidence that the ML pipeline, including the model itself, is working correctly. There are a few ways to do this.

15.2.1 Run-through data

The purpose of run-though data is simply to verify that every part of the ML pipeline connects properly and functions without breaking. This data set should consist of the smallest amount of data for which the pipeline and model is able to function correctly. The small size means that it should be quick to run through the pipeline (seconds or minutes at most), which enables you to identify and fix any issues quickly. The last thing you want to do is run your pipeline on the real training data set for two and a half days, only for it to fail because of a trivial typo somewhere in the code. That is what the run-through data is for – to catch errors quickly.

15.2.2 Synthetic data

The purpose of synthetic data is to validate that the model exploits predictability when it is present, and also that it does *not* invent predictability when it is *not* present. To do this we create two synthetic data sets. The first adds the target variable to the list of predictive features (which is *not* something we should generally do!). The purpose of this *maximally informative data set* is to verify that the model is able to take advantage of the perfect predictor – the actual target variable. Model performance should be extremely (unrealistically) high. If it is not, that suggests a problem somewhere in the pipeline. The second takes the real data but replaces the target value with random noise. This is the *zero information data set*. It should be impossible to predict truly random noise. If your model appears to be able to do so nonetheless, that is a warning sign. (This approach is sometimes referred to as a *placebo test*.)

15.2.3   Trivial models

For binary classification tasks, create models that predict (1) always true, (2) always false and (3) a randomly chosen true or false prediction in proportion to true and false in the training data. Your final model should do better than any of these trivial models to represent a true improvement. For regression tasks, create models that predict (1) zero always, (2) the average of the target variable in the training data. Again, your final model should do better than these trivial models.

15.2.4   Simple benchmark models

Create a simple tree predictor with a maximum tree depth of 3 and a simple LASSO model. These are reasonably simplistic ML approaches that should be easy to beat with more sophisticated approaches. If a more sophisticated approach cannot beat these simple models, there may be an issue in the way the more sophisticated model is set up or trained. As a bonus, these simple benchmark models will highlight the most useful, predictive features in your data set. This can be very helpful in informing additional feature engineering efforts.

15.2.5   Current approach

If the current approach to solving the task is already formalized, it can be useful to treat it as a model. Perhaps the current approach uses a specific set of rules, or a formula, or a flow chart. If so, convert it into a model (with code) and calculate its performance measure. Obviously, any replacement model should do better than the current approach. This way it is possible to quantify the improvement due to the new model directly.

15.3 Model development

Once you are confident that the model pipeline is working properly and you have a set of benchmarks to beat, it is time to focus on getting the best out of your selected ML approach. In practical terms, this means hyper-parameter tuning. For many people hyper-parameter tuning means finding the optimal settings for the many "dials and switches" that can be set for a particular ML approach. And those "dials and switches" are certainly hyper-parameters. *But so is any choice that you make by reference to whether it improves performance on the validation data.* When you are "trying out" something, it is strictly speaking hyper-parameter tuning. Should you interact two features to create a third? That is a hyper-parameter, if you choose based on validation data performance. Should you include a dimensionality reduction step in your data pipeline? Ditto.

If you decide to do something without checking whether it improves performance, then strictly speaking it is no longer a hyper-parameter. For instance the decision to add a scaling step to your data pipeline to support a neural network model (which requires scaled data) is not in itself a hyper-parameter. However if you try out a scaling step to see if it improves performance, then it becomes a hyper-parameter. Seen this way model development and hyper-parameter tuning are equivalent terms. In practice many people use the term hyper-parameter tuning in the narrow sense of picking the best setting on the "dials and switches" of a particular ML approach.

Hyper-parameter tuning can be automated. In its simplest incarnation, you can simply write code to try out a range of different values for a specific hyper-parameter and record the performance of the model on validation data for each choice of hyper-parameter. You then retain the choice of hyper-parameter with the best performance. This approach can be extended to choices about data preparation by packaging both the data preparation steps and the model into a "super-model" in which choices about the data preparation are also hyper-parameters.

The automated approach quickly runs into problems when faced with the dozens of plausible hyper-parameters, each of which could take on dozens of plausible values themselves. In fact, if you have a dozen hyper-parameters and for each hyper-parameter you have ten plausible values, the total number of models to train and evaluate is $10^{12} = 1,000,000,000,000$; this number is better known as a trillion. If you (optimistically) assume that you can train and evaluate a model in 1 second flat, it will still take you around 38 thousand years check every single combination of plausible hyper parameters. Clearly this is not a feasible approach.

In practice, the problem is addressed by focusing on a smaller set of hyper-parameters and potential hyper-parameter values. For instance testing four hyper-parameters for each of five values requires training $5^4 = 625$ models. This will take just over 10 hours if your model trains and evaluates in around a minute. You can simply run the hyper-parameter tuning code over night while you are sleeping.

It is a good idea to play around with different hyper-parameter choices "by hand" for a couple of hours. This can help identify the hyper-parameters that are most influential and the realistic ranges for different hyper parameters. It is also helpful to look at the choices other people made for hyper-parameters using similar ML approaches on similar problems. The purpose of this activity is *not* to select the best hyper-parameters, but rather to identify the best combination of hyper-parameters and values to explore.

To select the best hyper-parameters, it may be best to rely on a specialized package that supports automated hyper-parameter tuning, such as Optuna.[2] The most recent hyper-parameter tuning packages incorporate some very sophisticated mathematical approaches to efficiently search for the most promising combination of hyper-parameters. In addition, it is automated – you can kick of the search on a Friday afternoon and come back to see what looks promising the next Monday. Finally, it is possible to parallelize the search across many computers. If you have a hundred computers available (for instance by renting them from a cloud computing platform) you can reduce the time to search hyper-parameters by close to 100 times.

Like most endeavors, hyper-parameter tuning yields diminishing marginal returns. The first 10% of tuning is likely to provide 95% of the total improvement achieved. How much effort you expend on hyper-parameter tuning therefore depends on how much value you expect from the incremental model performance.

15.4 Performance vs value

Trying to wring the last fraction of a decimal point out of a performance measure can become an obsession. But it should not. There is rarely much difference, in practical terms, between a model with an RMSE of 14.7 and one with an RMSE of 14.5. The same goes for the difference between an

R-squared measure of 98.1% and 98.3%. Unless that extra performance *really* matters, the effort is probably better spent on more mundane matters such as data integrity or proper error reporting. Keep in mind that when you keep evaluating different hyper-parameters, you are in some sense "fitting" the hyper-parameters of the overall ML system to the validation data set. This is not that dissimilar to fitting the model parameters to the training data. Just as you can overfit the training data, you can also overfit the validation data with obsessive hyper-parameter tuning. (This is why you need test data for an unbiased estimate of performance on *new* data.) The reality is that you will probably end up losing that hard-won but tiny improvement on the validation data set when you bring the model to bear on new data.

The same observation applies to model complexity. From a business perspective, a 500% relative increase in complexity rarely justifies a 1% relative improvement in performance. The more complex a model is, the more opportunities there are for mistakes, the harder it is to understand and the more resources are required to keep it running smoothly in production. Complexity drives both performance and cost. For that reason, the highly visible increase in performance must be balanced against the often-hidden costs of complexity.

15.5   Technical debt

If you have ever borrowed money from a bank, you understand the concept of debt. Sometimes it is useful to be able to spend more money than you have, and then repay it later. There is an equivalent in domestic life. When you are pressed for time, you can usually find extra time by deferring your usual responsibilities (cleaning and tidying, mowing the lawn, answering emails, doing shopping, and so on.) However, this extra time is not free, because eventually you will have to attend to these responsibilities. In other words, you can "borrow" time from your domestic responsibilities, but eventually you will have to pay it back, possibly with interest.

The same concept exists in systems development, where it goes by the name of *technical debt*. In systems development there is usually a proper way to do things, and a quick way. The quick way saves you time in the short run, but eventually costs you much more time in the long run. This ability to take short cuts in systems development is technical debt. If you do not at some future point take the time to do things properly, you will end up with a system that is so full of short cuts and other expediencies that it becomes very hard to maintain. At some point, the expected time and cost for any meaningful change to the system rapidly approaches the time and cost of rebuilding the system from scratch (which happens often enough).

The problem with technical debt is that it tends to be glaringly obvious to technical developers, but completely invisible to non-technical managers. Adding functionality to a system the quick way and the proper way both yields a system that implements the functionality. But when you keep taking the quick way, the cost of adding additional functionality to the system further down the line increases exponentially. A workshop is a good analogy. If you do not put tools back in their proper places, you save a bit of time initially. But pretty soon you will be spending most of your time looking for tools, rather than doing any work. When developers complain about technical debt, they mean that the system has become so untidy because of all the previous short-cuts that it is now becoming hard to get any work done. As a result it is necessary to spend time to tidy things; this is called *refactoring* by software developers. Technical debt is real; just like financial borrowing, it might be useful to get through a tough stretch, as long as you don't forget to pay it back in full and on time.

Notes

1   See https://github.com/torvalds/linux. At the time of writing, the project had 13,464 contributors and (roughly) 27.8 million lines of code.
2   See https://optuna.org/.

16 Deployment and monitoring

Deployment is a crucial step in the ML lifecycle. When things go wrong in deployment, it tends to go wrong in very expensive and highly visible ways. In this chapter we'll discuss the key steps involved in deploying an ML system, along with a few suggestions for identifying and mitigating potential risks.

16.1 Set up the production environment

The first step in deployment is setting up the production environment. Most production systems are based on servers hosted either on-premises or in the cloud. Production servers are optimized and configured for high reliability and stable throughput. As a general rule, the set-up in the production system should mirror that used in development. (It might be easier to set up the development system to mirror the target production system, rather than the other way round) Differences in the set-up between the development system and the production system can lead to the emergence of new and unforeseen issues.

Over the past decade or so *containers* have become a common approach to enforce consistency in production environments. A container is a collection of data that fully describes a particular server configuration (the operating system, any installed software and their associated dependencies, environmental variables, and so forth).[1] Containers can be executed on different hardware platforms, but from the perspective of software running *inside* the container it all looks identical.

DOI: 10.4324/9781003330929-18

16.2   Connect the plumbing

Once the production environment is set up the next step is configuring connectivity to other processes that interact with the ML system. In general an ML system will be set up to make predictions using supplied data. If the typical workload is based on single requests for predictions, this interface might be best structured as an API (application programming interface).

These days it is common for APIs to operate over networks, borrowing the infrastructure of the internet. A typical API will consist of a *request* delivered via HTTP (e.g. https://www.mytemp.com/temp?city=berlin) with the *response* delivered as a structured text file in JSON or XML format (e.g. {"City": "Berlin", "Temp": 19, "Units": "Celsius"}). The use of APIs supports the best practice of structuring software as a logically distinct modules communicating via defined interfaces (see Section 15.1). Do be aware that when dealing with a large number of prediction requests it might be necessary to scale to multiple servers to service the load. This entails additional complexity (persistent queues, load-balancers, automatic fail-over, etc.) which requires a set of skills different from that possessed by the typical data scientist.

It is more efficient to process prediction requests in batches rather than one-by-one. If this is feasible, then predictions requests can be grouped in a file to be processed by the ML system on a regular basis. Individual prediction is best suited to situations where down-stream systems require the prediction to function (e.g. loan approvals, online vendor recommender systems). Batch processing may be appropriate when periodic updates are feasible (e.g. weather forecasting, asset allocation decisions).

In addition to accepting prediction requests and providing predictions, there is another bit of plumbing that is essential, but often neglected – status reporting. Production systems should continuously report their current status to a central dashboard that is continuously monitored. The actual reporting may vary, but conceptually we can distinguish between green (working correctly), orange (degraded performance or non-critical errors) and red (critical errors, service unavailable). Cloud computing providers typically provide a public summary view across their products.[2] Error reporting should be detailed enough to understand what the problem is (hardware failure, network connectivity lost, out-of-memory, etc.). Error reporting and logs should ideally be recorded on a separate machine so that it remains available even if the server itself becomes unresponsive. (Error reporting and logs are not helpful for resolving a problem if they cannot be accessed!)

16.3   Test, test, test

Once the production environment is set up and connected, it should be tested. Testing on a production server is complicated by the fact that it is by design connected to other production systems. Test data accidentally entering downstream production systems can lead to a host of issues that are best avoided! One approach is to replace connectivity to downstream production systems with specially constructed test systems. These test systems interact with the ML system following the exact protocol used by the normal production systems, but instead of acting on any information flows it simply records them in a repository to be checked for correctness. The same approach can be used to create up-stream systems to feed test data to the ML system.

A further benefit of this approach is that it may be possible to connect the development version of the ML system to the same test systems. The recorded downstream information flows can then be compared between the ML system hosted in the production environment and the ML system hosted in the development environment. If all is well the information flows should be identical; if not, something is clearly amiss and should be investigated.

16.4   Flip the switch

At some point the ML system needs to go live and enter production; this is the endpoint of the deployment process. If all goes well, it just works. If not, well, you have a problem. And the biggest problem you have is that problems in a live production system creates time pressure, urgency, a lot of shouting – and a tendency for people to panic and make things worse. The ideal way to side-step this problem is to build a system that is simply incapable of going wrong and then test it with the firm conviction that it is wrong. But let's be realistic; there is *always* a risk that something will go wrong on the big day. So it is only prudent to have a plan B. One sensible approach is to set up a fallback system that automatically kicks in if you pull the plug on the new ML system. If the ML system replaces an existing system, you can fall back to that system. (If it was acceptable before, presumably it remains acceptable.) An alternative is to have in place a manual system, if the volume of requests permit. If it is new functionality, you can present it as a "beta" product that is still under development. If the system fails on deployment, you can simply put up a webpage explaining that the system is down for maintenance.

Before deployment, everyone involved should have the names, responsibilities and cell-phone numbers of everyone else involved. A specific person should be designated as the contact for reporting issues. This person should have sufficient technical experience to understand what has gone wrong and what the implications are, be sufficiently involved in the project to know who is responsible for what and have enough organizational seniority to give instructions. (The project lead is a natural candidate for this role. Knowing that they will have to handle any issues on the day might also encourage them to work hard to ensure it all goes smoothly!).

Lastly, there is a time and place for everything. Do *not* deploy a system at 4:25 pm on a Friday. By the time it is clear that something is wrong it will be 6:18 pm and your engineering staff will be stuck in commuting traffic. At 10:42 am the next Saturday – when you are trying desperately to contain cascading failures – the one network engineer that could solve the root problem will out of reach on a ski-slope, in a fishing boat or in a basement rave somewhere. Be sensible and deploy your system like the pro's: at 10:30 am on a Tuesday.

16.5   Continuous monitoring

Just because the ML system is deployed and working great does not mean that the work is complete. Like all IT systems, the ML system needs to be monitored continuously to ensure it is working. This is harder than you might expect. Unlike other systems, an ML system might *seem* like it is working when in fact it is not. If accuracy drops from 98.9% in the first week to 98.2% in the next week, what does that mean? It could simply be part of the natural variability in performance that should be expected. Or it could be because one of the data feeds have quietly died, leaving stale data to be fed into the ML system. The fundamental issue is that it is not possible to say conclusively whether an ML system is operating correctly *only* by looking at its performance. Certainly, a large and sudden drop in performance is an indication that something is amiss, and for this reason model performance should definitely be among the metrics that are being monitored. But the impact on model performance from problems such as stale data might be lost in the natural variability that should be expected in day-to-day performance. It might be a few weeks before you can be sure something is wrong, and that assumes that you are actively checking for issues.

There is no perfect solution to this problem, but you can improve the chances of detecting issues early by performing the following checks:

1. Record model performance and compare it with (a) the test-data result from the final model and (b) the average performance of the model over the past day, week, or month. (Granted, this one is obvious, but I list it here for the sake of completeness.)

2. If possible, also record feature importance results (such as SHAP values – see Section 9.3). Large changes in feature importance might be symptomatic of problems with data, which should be fixed. Alternatively, large changes in feature importance might be real, and signal that the distribution of data in the production environment has deviated significantly from the data used in training. If might be necessary to re-train the model to better reflect the distribution of data encountered in the production environment.

3. Set up a side-model to predict the *errors* of the ML system with the same input data used by the ML system. As a rule, model errors should not be predictable to any significant degree using the same input data. If model errors *are* predictable, this suggests that the ML system could be improved by retraining the model with new data (and possibly with a more powerful and flexible ML approach).

4. Report model errors by the ranges of other variables such as day-of-the week, calendar month, transaction amount, customer activity, etc. Then look for significant *changes* in these patterns over time.

5. Manually review a selection of predictions on a periodic basis. Sometime problems invisible to software are blindingly obvious to a human. A variable that *cannot* be missing is somehow missing. A variable that should contain a date contains a dollar amount (or vice versa). A shipping distance is listed as $-95,293,523,320,291$ miles (did you remember to check for *negative* shipping distances in your data validation code? How about shipping distances that are roughly 100 times the distance to the sun?).

6. Check the input variables in the data feeds. If the maximum and minimum of a particular variable is the same for some length of time (say a week), that variable has probably gone stale. If an input variable has a correlation of 1 or −1 with another input variable, they are probably duplicates of the same data. If an input variable is 100% missing for a week, that likely indicates a problem.

7. For batch processes, check the dates on the input files (the X's) and the ML system predictions (the $\hat{y}$'s). When process information flow is via files (and it often is), the downstream system might happily continue to consume a predictions file created 2 months ago, just before the actual ML system ceased making predictions because someone in accounts failed to pay the cloud service provider where the ML model was hosted. (Are you *sure* this could never happen in your organization?)

8. Even if none of the issues above happen, the performance of the ML system will inevitably deteriorate over time. The world is continuously changing, often in small and subtle ways. However, these small changes compound until 9 years later the data flowing through the ML system is no longer the same as when the model was last trained 9 years earlier. This not a mistake in data feeds, or the ML model. The world has simply changed, and no-one told the ML system. This is the familiar *data-drift* issue we discussed earlier. The cure is retraining the model on more recent data.

16.6   Final thoughts

This chapter concludes our journey. In this book we covered the essentials of ML (Part I) and discussed some important aspects of implementing ML systems in organizations (Part II). Perhaps this might be a good time to revisit the 34 lines of Python in Figure 1.1 that we used to introduce ML. The difference is that you now understand *what* the code is doing, but just as importantly, *why* it is doing it.

I do hope you have found the book a useful introduction to ML. All the best for your future ML projects. Do let me know how it went – the good, the bad and the ugly! You can reach me at p.geertsema@auckland.ac.nz (if that fails, try a Google search).

Notes

1   Docker Engine (https://www.docker.com) is an example of software that operates containers. In large enterprises specialized software is used for the *orchestration* of containers, that is deploying, managing and networking multiple containers. Kubernetes (https://kubernetes.io/) is an example of software that handles orchestration.

2   For examples see https://health.aws.amazon.com/health/status, https://status.azure.com/en-gb/status and https://status.cloud.google.com/.

Index

Note: **Bold** page numbers refer to tables; *Italic* page numbers refer to figures and page numbers followed by "n" denote endnotes

A/B testing 118
abstraction 3, 138
accuracy 5, 12, 24, 30, 54–56, 63, 128, *129*, 150
activated linear model 50, 51
activation function 49, 50, 53, 54
ad-hoc script code 115–116
adversarial data attack 109, *110*
agile approach 139
ANN 47
API 148
application programming interface 148
artificial general intelligence 86
Artificial Intelligence 6
artificial neural networks 47
attack surface 109
attention mechanism 83
AUC 30, 64–66
augmentation strategy 122
autoencoder 74

back-propagation 52
base category 39
batch gradient descent 52
batch training 17–18
Bengio, Yoshua 48
bias 35, 48–52, 67, 111
big data 7
big-bang approach 139
blockchain 6, 7
boosting 10, 56, 67–69, 90, 135
Brahe, Tycho 6
business case 100, 101, 103, 133; cost savings 124; executive summary

126; project description 127; project benefits 127–129, *129*; proof-of-concept 129–130; resources 130; stakeholders 125; technical appendix 130–132

categorical cross-entropy loss function 54
categorical feature 20
causal machine learning 86
central processing units 9–10
classification **15**, 28–30, 64, 76, 81; logistic regression 42–43
classification task 15, 18n1, 20, 38, 42, 54; binary 142; confusion matrices 62–63, **62**; performance measures 63–64; ROC-AUC measure 64–67, *65–66*; thresholds 64–67, *65–66*;
clustering **15**, 72, 79n2; HAC 75–78, *76*, *78*; k-means 75
clusters 75–77, *76*
CNN 10, 56, 81
coefficient(s) 34, 35, 40, 43–44, 45n6
Computer Science 6, 7
confusion matrix 62–63, **62**, 65
constant 34, 35, 92, 114, 121
containers 147
continuous features 19
continuous monitoring 150–152
convolutional neural network 10, 56, 81, *83*
correlation heatmap 77
correlation matrix 28, 45n8, 77
correlation measures 28
CPUs 9–10

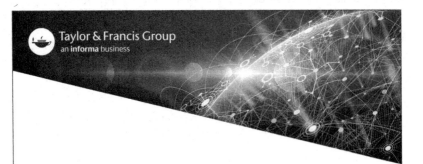